COPPER SKILLET

COOK WITH YOUR FAVORITE PAN IN THE KITCHEN

pil

Publications International, Ltd.

Pictured on the front cover: Skillet Lasagna with Vegetables *(page 102).*
Pictured on the back cover *(clockwise from top left):* Couscous Primavera *(page 136),* Cinnamon Roll-Topped Peach and Raspberry Cobbler *(page 159),* Chicken Nuggets with Spicy Tomato Dipping Sauce *(page 48)* and Ham and Vegetable Omelet *(page 24).*

ISBN: 978-1-64030-019-4

Manufactured in China.

8 7 6 5 4 3 2 1

Microwave Cooking: Microwave ovens vary in wattage. Use the cooking times as guidelines and check for doneness before adding more time.

CONTENTS

BREAKFAST FAVORITES

CRANBERRY BUTTERMILK PANCAKES

MAKES 18 (3-INCH) PANCAKES (ABOUT 6 SERVINGS)

1 cup all-purpose flour

1 cup whole wheat flour

2 teaspoons baking powder

1 teaspoon baking soda

½ teaspoon ground cinnamon

¼ teaspoon ground nutmeg

⅔ cup whole berry cranberry sauce, divided

2 eggs

2 tablespoons vegetable oil

1½ cups buttermilk

Maple syrup (optional)

1. Combine all-purpose flour, whole wheat flour, baking powder, baking soda, cinnamon and nutmeg in small bowl; mix well. Whisk cranberry sauce, eggs and oil in large bowl until well blended. Gradually stir in flour mixture until combined. Stir in buttermilk until smooth and well blended.

2. Heat large skillet over medium heat. Pour ¼ cupfuls of batter 2 inches apart into skillet. Cook 3 minutes or until lightly browned and edges begin to bubble. Turn over; cook 3 minutes or until lightly browned. Repeat with remaining batter. Serve with syrup, if desired.

PEA AND SPINACH FRITTATA

MAKES 4 SERVINGS

1 cup chopped onion

¼ cup water

1 cup frozen peas

1 cup fresh spinach

6 egg whites

2 eggs

½ cup cooked brown rice

¼ cup milk

2 tablespoons grated Romano or Parmesan cheese, plus additional for garnish

1 tablespoon chopped fresh mint *or* 1 teaspoon dried mint, crushed

¼ teaspoon black pepper

⅛ teaspoon salt

1. Combine onion and water in large skillet; bring to a boil over high heat. Reduce heat to medium. Cover; cook 2 to 3 minutes or until onion is tender. Stir in peas; cook until heated through. Drain. Add spinach; cook and stir 1 minute or until spinach just begins to wilt.

2. Combine egg whites, eggs, rice, milk, 2 tablespoons Romano cheese, mint, pepper and salt in medium bowl. Add egg mixture to skillet. Cook, without stirring, 2 minutes or until eggs begin to set. Run large spoon around edge of skillet, lifting eggs for even cooking. Remove skillet from heat when eggs are almost set but surface is still moist.

3. Cover; let stand 3 to 4 minutes or until surface is set. Sprinkle with additional Romano cheese, if desired. Cut into four wedges to serve.

TURKEY AND BACON MINI WAFFLEWICHES

MAKES 2 SERVINGS

1 teaspoon Dijon mustard

1 teaspoon honey

8 frozen mini waffles
(2 pieces, divided into
individual waffles)

2 thin slices deli turkey, cut
into thin strips

2 tablespoons cooked and
crumbled bacon

4 teaspoons shredded
Cheddar or mozzarella
cheese

2 teaspoons butter

1. Combine mustard and honey in small bowl. Spread small amount of mustard mixture onto one side of 4 waffles. Top evenly with turkey and bacon; sprinkle with cheese. Top with 4 remaining waffles.

2. Melt butter in medium skillet over medium heat. Pressing with back of spatula, cook sandwiches 3 to 4 minutes per side or until cheese is melted and waffles are golden brown.

FIRE & ICE BRUNCH SKILLET

MAKES 4 SERVINGS

1 (6.8-ounce) package RICE-A-RONI® Spanish Rice

2 tablespoons margarine or butter

1 (16-ounce) jar salsa

⅓ cup sour cream

¼ cup thinly sliced green onions

4 large eggs

1 cup (4 ounces) shredded Cheddar cheese

Chopped cilantro (optional)

1. In large skillet over medium heat, sauté rice-vermicelli mix with margarine until vermicelli is golden brown.

2. Slowly stir in 2 cups water, salsa and Special Seasonings; bring to a boil. Reduce heat to low. Cover; simmer 15 to 20 minutes or until rice is tender.

3. Stir in sour cream and green onions. Using large spoon, make 4 indentations in rice mixture. Break 1 egg into each indentation. Reduce heat to low. Cover; cook 8 minutes or until eggs are cooked to desired doneness.

4. Sprinkle cheese evenly over eggs and rice. Cover; let stand 3 minutes or until cheese is melted. Sprinkle with cilantro, if desired.

TIP: A twist on Mexican-style huevos rancheros, serve this for brunch or as a light dinner.

TOASTED MONKEY SANDWICHES

MAKES 2 SERVINGS

¼ cup SKIPPY® Creamy
  Peanut Butter

4 slices cinnamon raisin,
  white or whole wheat
  bread

1 medium banana, sliced

1. Evenly spread SKIPPY® Creamy Peanut Butter on 2 slices bread, then top with banana and remaining bread slices.

2. Cook sandwiches in 12-inch nonstick skillet sprayed with nonstick cooking spray over medium heat until golden brown, about 4 minutes, turning once.

TIP: Try with Skippy® Natural Creamy Peanut Butter Spread with Honey!

SAUSAGE AND RED PEPPER STRATA

MAKES 4 SERVINGS

6 ounces bulk breakfast pork sausage

½ teaspoon dried oregano

¼ teaspoon red pepper flakes (optional)

4 slices day-old French bread, cut into ½-inch cubes

½ medium red bell pepper, finely chopped

¼ cup chopped fresh parsley, plus additional for garnish

4 eggs

1 cup evaporated milk

1 teaspoon Dijon mustard

¼ teaspoon black pepper

½ cup (2 ounces) shredded sharp Cheddar cheese

1. Heat 8-inch square skillet over medium-high heat. Add sausage, oregano and red pepper flakes, if desired; cook and stir 6 to 8 minutes or until sausage is browned, stirring to break up meat. Drain fat.

2. Wipe skillet clean; line bottom with bread cubes. Sprinkle sausage mixture evenly over bread cubes; top evenly with bell pepper and ¼ cup parsley.

3. Whisk eggs, evaporated milk, mustard and black pepper in medium bowl until well blended. Pour egg mixture over sausage. Cover tightly with foil; refrigerate 8 hours or overnight.

4. Preheat oven to 350°F. Bake, covered, 55 minutes.

5. Remove foil. Sprinkle with cheese; bake 5 minutes or until cheese is melted. Garnish with additional parsley. Cut into four pieces before serving.

MEXED-UP FRENCH TOAST WITH SPICED CHOCOLATE DRIZZLE

MAKES 4 SERVINGS

6 eggs, beaten

½ cup half-and-half or milk

1 packet (1.25 ounces) ORTEGA® Taco Seasoning Mix or 40% Less Sodium Taco Seasoning Mix, divided

8 slices Texas toast-style bread, thawed if frozen

2 tablespoons butter

1 cup semisweet chocolate chips

¼ cup whipping cream

Maple Grove Farms® maple syrup

COMBINE eggs, half-and-half and 2 tablespoons seasoning mix in shallow bowl or pie pan; mix well.

PLACE bread slices in egg mixture, allowing bread to absorb mixture before turning to coat other side.

HEAT about ½ tablespoon butter in large skillet over medium heat. Place 2 egg-coated bread slices in skillet; cook about 4 minutes or until golden brown. Turn slices over and cook 4 minutes or until golden brown. Transfer to serving plate. Repeat with remaining butter and bread slices.

PLACE chocolate chips and remaining seasoning mix in small microwavable bowl. Microwave on HIGH 30 seconds; stir. Repeat as necessary until chips are melted and mixture is smooth. Stir in cream; mix well.

DRIZZLE chocolate mixture over French toast and serve with maple syrup.

TIP: If you can't find Texas toast in the bread section or freezer case, you can use day-old thick-cut white sandwich bread to make your own Texas toast.

TURKEY MIGAS

MAKES 6 SERVINGS

10 large eggs

1 teaspoon chili powder

¼ cup (½ stick) butter

1 cup onion, cut into 1½×¼-inch strips

1 cup green bell pepper, cut into 1½×¼-inch strips

1 cup red bell pepper, cut into 1½×¼-inch strips

2 cups diced leftover cooked BUTTERBALL® Turkey

1 cup (4 ounces) shredded pepper jack cheese

4 ounces corn chips

20 fresh cilantro leaves

1 cup prepared chunky salsa

1. Beat eggs with chili powder in medium bowl; set aside.

2. Melt butter in medium skillet over medium-high heat. Add onion and bell peppers; cook and stir 2 to 3 minutes or until crisp-tender.

3. Add turkey and egg mixture; stir well. Reduce heat to medium. When eggs begin to set, draw heatproof spatula along bottom and sides of skillet to loosen eggs. Stir in cheese. Continue to loosen cooked eggs from bottom and sides of skillet. Gently fold in corn chips. Continue cooking until egg mixture is set.

4. Spoon onto serving platter. Sprinkle with cilantro; pour salsa down center.

HAM AND POTATO PANCAKES

MAKES 16 PANCAKES

¾ pound Yukon Gold potatoes, peeled, grated and squeezed dry (about 2 cups)

¼ cup finely chopped green onions

2 eggs, beaten

1 cup (4 to 5 ounces) finely chopped cooked ham

¼ cup rice flour

¼ teaspoon salt

¼ teaspoon black pepper

2 to 3 tablespoons vegetable oil

Chili sauce or fruit chutney (optional)

1. Combine potatoes, green onions and eggs in large bowl; mix well. Add ham, rice flour, salt and pepper; mix well.

2. Heat 2 tablespoons oil in large skillet over medium-high heat. Drop batter into skillet by heaping tablespoonfuls and press with back of spoon to flatten. Cook 2 to 3 minutes per side. Remove to paper towels to drain. Add remaining 1 tablespoon oil, if necessary, to cook remaining batter. Serve pancakes with chili sauce.

TIP: Rice flour can often be substituted for regular all-purpose flour in recipes like this one. If a small amount of flour is called for to bind ingredients together, rice flour works just as well as regular all-purpose flour. Use either brown or white rice flour. Brown rice flour, like the brown rice it is made from, has a slightly better nutritional profile.

LEMON-POPPY SEED FRENCH TOAST WITH BLUEBERRY SAUCE

MAKES 4 SERVINGS

6 slices whole wheat sandwich bread

Blueberry Sauce (recipe follows)

2 eggs

1 egg white

⅓ cup milk

2 teaspoons grated lemon peel

½ teaspoon poppy seeds

½ teaspoon vanilla

Nonstick cooking spray

1. Cut bread slices in half. Prepare Blueberry Sauce.

2. Combine eggs, egg white, milk, lemon peel, poppy seeds and vanilla in large shallow dish; whisk to combine.

3. Place bread in dish; turn to coat until egg mixture is absorbed.

4. Coat large skillet with nonstick cooking spray; heat over medium heat. Add 2 bread slices to skillet; cook, turning once, 2 to 3 minutes per side or until lightly browned. Repeat with remaining bread slices.

5. Serve toast topped with Blueberry Sauce.

BLUEBERRY SAUCE

MAKES ABOUT 1 CUP

1¾ cups fresh or frozen
blueberries, divided

¼ cup water, divided

2 teaspoons cornstarch

1. Combine 1½ cups berries and 2 tablespoons water in medium saucepan. Cook over medium heat, uncovered and stirring occasionally, 4 to 5 minutes or until berries are softened and mixture is hot and bubbly.

2. Combine remaining 2 tablespoons water and cornstarch in small bowl, stirring until cornstarch dissolves. Gradually stir into blueberry mixture. Cook, stirring occasionally, about 1 minute or until slightly thickened. Remove from heat. Stir in remaining ¼ cup blueberries.

SKILLET SAUSAGE WITH POTATOES AND ROSEMARY

MAKES 4 TO 6 SERVINGS

1 tablespoon vegetable oil

3 cups diced red skin potatoes

1 cup diced onion

1 pound BOB EVANS® Original Recipe Roll Sausage

½ teaspoon dried rosemary

¼ teaspoon rubbed sage

Salt and black pepper to taste

2 tablespoons chopped fresh parsley

Heat oil in large skillet over medium-high heat 1 minute. Add potatoes; cook 5 to 10 minutes or until slightly brown, stirring occasionally. Add onion; cook until tender. Add crumbled sausage; cook until browned. Add rosemary, sage, salt and pepper; cook and stir until well blended. Transfer to serving platter and garnish with parsley. Refrigerate leftovers.

HAM AND VEGETABLE OMELET

MAKES 4 SERVINGS

2 ounces (about ½ cup) diced ham

1 small onion, diced

½ medium green bell pepper, diced

½ medium red bell pepper, diced

2 cloves garlic, minced

6 eggs

⅛ teaspoon black pepper

½ cup (2 ounces) shredded Colby cheese, divided

1 medium tomato, chopped

Hot pepper sauce (optional)

1. Heat large skillet over medium-high heat. Add ham, onion, bell peppers and garlic; cook and stir 5 minutes or until vegetables are crisp-tender. Transfer mixture to large bowl.

2. Wipe out skillet with paper towels; heat over medium-high heat. Pour eggs into skillet; sprinkle with black pepper. Cook 2 minutes or until bottom is set, lifting edge of egg with spatula to allow uncooked portion to flow underneath. Reduce heat to medium-low; cover and cook 4 minutes or until top is set.

3. Gently slide omelet onto large serving plate; spoon ham mixture down center. Sprinkle with ¼ cup cheese. Carefully fold two sides of omelet over ham mixture; sprinkle with remaining ¼ cup cheese and tomato. Cut into four wedges; serve immediately with hot pepper sauce, if desired.

SWEET POTATO AND TURKEY SAUSAGE HASH

MAKES 2 SERVINGS

1 mild or hot turkey Italian sausage link (about 4 ounces)

1 small red onion, finely chopped

1 small red bell pepper, finely chopped

1 small sweet potato, peeled and cut into ½-inch cubes

¼ teaspoon salt

¼ teaspoon black pepper

⅛ teaspoon ground cumin

⅛ teaspoon chipotle chili powder

1. Remove sausage from casings; discard casings. Shape sausage into ½-inch balls. Heat large skillet over medium heat. Add sausage; cook and stir 3 to 5 minutes or until browned. Remove from skillet; set aside.

2. Add onion, bell pepper, sweet potato, salt, black pepper, cumin and chili powder to same skillet; cook and stir 5 to 8 minutes or until sweet potato is tender.

3. Stir in sausage; cook without stirring 5 minutes or until hash is lightly browned.

ANDOUILLE SAUSAGE CAJUN SCRAMBLE

MAKES 2 SERVINGS

½ package (13.5 ounces) JOHNSONVILLE® Andouille Fully Cooked Sausage

6 large eggs, beaten

1 teaspoon Cajun seasoning

2 to 3 tablespoons olive oil

1 small red potato, cut into ¼-inch dice

1 small onion, chopped

½ cup chopped green bell pepper

½ cup shredded pepper jack cheese

½ cup salsa (optional)

1. Cut sausage link diagonally into ¼-inch slices; set aside. Whisk together eggs and Cajun seasoning in medium bowl; set aside.

2. Heat 2 tablespoons oil in large nonstick skillet over medium-low heat until hot. Add potato; cook and stir 5 minutes. Increase heat to medium. Add onion and bell pepper; cook and stir 5 minutes or until vegetables are lightly browned. Add sausage slices; cook and stir 2 to 3 minutes. If skillet seems dry, add remaining 1 tablespoon oil and heat.

3. Pour egg mixture into skillet; cook without stirring 1 minute. Gently bring edges of mixture to center, allowing uncooked egg mixture to reach pan bottom. Continue cooking and folding to blend ingredients. When eggs are still moist but almost cooked through, add cheese. Cook and fold 30 to 45 seconds or until cheese has melted.

4. Divide evenly between two plates; top evenly with salsa, if desired. Serve immediately.

SERVING SUGGESTION: Serve with buttered sourdough bread for a hearty breakfast.

APPLE MONTE CRISTOS

MAKES 2 SANDWICHES

4 ounces Gouda cheese, shredded

1 ounce cream cheese, softened

2 teaspoons honey

½ teaspoon ground cinnamon

4 slices cinnamon raisin bread

1 small apple, cored and thinly sliced

¼ cup milk

1 egg, beaten

1 tablespoon butter

Powdered sugar

1. Combine Gouda cheese, cream cheese, honey and cinnamon in small bowl; stir until well blended. Spread cheese mixture evenly on all bread slices. Layer apple slices evenly over cheese on 2 bread slices; top with remaining bread slices.

2. Combine milk and egg in shallow bowl; stir until well blended. Dip sandwiches in egg mixture, turning to coat well.

3. Melt butter in large skillet over medium heat. Add sandwiches; cook 4 to 5 minutes per side or until cheese is melted and sandwiches are golden brown. Sprinkle with powdered sugar.

TIP: Melting the butter in the skillet before adding the sandwiches adds additional buttery flavor.

ZUCCHINI-TOMATO FRITTATA

MAKES 4 SERVINGS

Nonstick olive oil-flavored cooking spray

1 cup sliced zucchini

1 cup broccoli florets

1 cup diced red or yellow bell pepper

3 whole eggs, lightly beaten*

5 egg whites, lightly beaten*

½ cup 1% low-fat cottage cheese

½ cup rehydrated sun-dried tomatoes (1 ounce dry), coarsely chopped**

¼ cup chopped green onions with tops

¼ cup chopped fresh basil

⅛ teaspoon ground red pepper

2 tablespoons grated Parmesan cheese

Paprika (optional)

*Or, substitute with cholesterol-free egg substitute to equal 6 large eggs.

**To rehydrate sun-dried tomatoes, pour 1 cup boiling water over tomatoes in small bowl. Let soak 5 to 10 minutes or until softened; drain well.

1. Preheat broiler. Spray 10-inch ovenproof skillet with cooking spray. Place zucchini, broccoli and bell pepper in skillet; cook and stir over high heat 3 to 4 minutes or until crisp-tender.

2. Combine whole eggs, egg whites, cottage cheese, tomatoes, green onions, basil and ground red pepper in medium bowl; mix well. Pour egg mixture over vegetables in skillet. Cook, uncovered, gently lifting sides of frittata so uncooked egg flows underneath. Cook 7 to 8 minutes or until frittata is almost firm and golden brown on bottom. Remove from heat. Sprinkle with Parmesan.

3. Broil about 5 inches from heat 3 to 5 minutes or until golden brown on surface. Garnish with paprika, if desired. Cut into four wedges. Serve immediately.

AMAZING APPETIZERS

CHICKEN BACON QUESADILLAS

MAKES 4 SERVINGS

4 teaspoons vegetable oil, divided

4 fajita-size tortillas (8-inch)

1 cup (4 ounces) shredded Colby-Jack cheese

2 cups coarsely chopped cooked chicken

4 slices bacon, crisp-cooked and coarsely chopped

½ cup pico de gallo

Salsa, sour cream and guacamole

1. Heat large nonstick skillet over medium heat; brush with 1 teaspoon oil. Place 1 tortilla in skillet; sprinkle with ¼ cup cheese. Spread ½ cup chicken over one half of tortilla; top with one fourth of bacon and 2 tablespoons pico de gallo.

2. Cook 1 to 2 minutes or until cheese is melted and bottom of tortilla is lightly browned. Fold tortilla over filling, pressing with spatula. Transfer to cutting board; cool slightly. Cut into wedges. Repeat with remaining ingredients. Serve with salsa, sour cream and guacamole.

BROCCOLI RAMEN FRITTERS WITH YOGURT DIPPING SAUCE

MAKES 8 FRITTERS

2 eggs

¼ cup all-purpose flour

1 package (3 ounces) ramen noodles, any flavor, cooked 1 minute and coarsely chopped

2 cups steamed broccoli, finely chopped

2 tablespoons vegetable oil

YOGURT DIPPING SAUCE

½ cup plain nonfat Greek yogurt

1 tablespoon lime juice

2 teaspoons olive oil

¼ teaspoon salt

1. Whisk together eggs, flour and seasoning packet from noodles in medium bowl. Add broccoli and chopped noodles; stir well.

2. Heat vegetable oil over medium-high heat in large skillet. Drop ¼ cupfuls broccoli mixture in skillet, careful not to crowd the pan. Cook 4 minutes, turn over, cook 3 minutes. Remove to plate; keep warm. Repeat with remaining vegetable oil and batter.

3. For Yogurt Dipping Sauce, combine yogurt, lime juice, olive oil and salt in small bowl; stir well. Serve with warm fritters.

FALAFEL NUGGETS

MAKES 12 SERVINGS

2 cans (about 15 ounces each) chickpeas

½ cup whole wheat flour

½ cup chopped fresh parsley

1 egg, beaten

⅓ cup lemon juice

¼ cup minced onion

2 tablespoons minced garlic

2 teaspoons ground cumin

½ teaspoon salt

½ teaspoon ground red pepper or red pepper flakes

Nonstick cooking spray

Marinara sauce

1. Drain chickpeas, reserving ¼ cup liquid. Combine chickpeas, reserved ¼ cup liquid, flour, parsley, egg, lemon juice, onion, garlic, cumin, salt and ground red pepper in food processor or blender; process until well blended. Shape into 36 (1-inch) balls; place 1 to 2 inches apart in large skillet. Refrigerate 15 minutes.

2. Meanwhile, preheat oven to 400°F.

3. Remove skillet from refrigerator. Spray nuggets lightly with cooking spray. Bake 15 to 20 minutes, turning once. Serve with warm marinara sauce.

SPICY CHICKEN BUNDLES

MAKES 12 APPETIZERS

1 pound ground chicken or turkey

2 teaspoons minced fresh ginger

2 cloves garlic, minced

¼ teaspoon red pepper flakes

3 tablespoons soy sauce

1 tablespoon cornstarch

1 tablespoon peanut or vegetable oil

⅓ cup finely chopped water chestnuts

⅓ cup thinly sliced green onions

¼ cup chopped peanuts

12 large lettuce leaves, such as romaine

Chinese hot mustard (optional)

1. Combine chicken, ginger, garlic and red pepper flakes in medium bowl. Blend soy sauce into cornstarch in cup until smooth.

2. Heat oil in large skillet over medium-high heat. Add chicken mixture; cook and stir 2 to 3 minutes until chicken is cooked through.

3. Stir soy sauce mixture; add to skillet. Cook and stir 30 seconds or until sauce boils and thickens. Add water chestnuts, green onions and peanuts; heat through.*

4. Divide filling evenly among lettuce leaves; roll up. Secure with toothpicks. Serve warm or at room temperature. Do not let filling stand at room temperature more than 2 hours. Serve with hot mustard.

Filling may be made ahead to this point; cover and refrigerate up to 4 hours. Reheat chicken filling until warm. Proceed as directed in step 4.

MAC & CHEESE BITES

MAKES ABOUT 2 DOZEN

3 packages (3 ounces each) ramen noodles, any flavor, divided*

8 ounces pasteurized process cheese product

1 cup (4 ounces) shredded Cheddar cheese

1 teaspoon salt

½ teaspoon ground red pepper

Vegetable oil

*Discard seasoning packets.

1. Prepare 2 packages ramen according to package directions; drain and return to saucepan.

2. Stir in cheese product, Cheddar cheese, salt and ground red pepper. Let stand 10 to 15 minutes.

3. Finely crush remaining packet ramen noodles in food processor or blender. Put crumbs in pie pan. Using hands, shape cheese mixture into 1-inch balls; roll in ramen crumbs. Flatten slightly.

4. Heat about ½ to 1 inch oil in large skillet. Add bites, a few at a time; cook 1½ minutes per side until golden brown. Remove from skillet; drain on paper towels.

FRIED PICKLE SPEARS

MAKES 12 SERVINGS

3 tablespoons all-purpose flour

1 teaspoon cornstarch

3 eggs

1 cup cornflake crumbs

12 pickle spears, patted dry

½ cup corn oil

Yellow mustard (optional)

1. Line serving dish with paper towels; set aside. Combine flour and cornstarch in small bowl. Beat eggs in another small bowl; set aside. Place cornflake crumbs in another small bowl.

2. Coat pickle spears in flour mixture, shaking off excess flour. Dip pickle in eggs; roll in cornflake crumbs. Repeat with remaining pickles.

3. Heat oil in large nonstick skillet over medium heat. Cook four pickles at a time, 1 to 2 minutes on each side or until golden brown. Remove to prepared serving dish. Repeat with remaining pickles. Serve with mustard, if desired.

QUICK CHICKEN QUESADILLAS

MAKES 8 APPETIZER OR 4 MAIN-DISH SERVINGS

4 boneless skinless chicken breasts

3 tablespoons vegetable oil, divided

½ teaspoon salt

1 large yellow onion, thinly sliced

8 (6- to 8-inch) flour tortillas

3 cups (12 ounces) shredded mild Cheddar or jack cheese

Salsa, sour cream and/or guacamole (optional)

1. Flatten chicken breasts and cut into 1×¼-inch strips.

2. Heat 2 tablespoons oil in large skillet. Add chicken and cook, stirring over high heat, 3 to 4 minutes or until lightly browned and cooked through. Season with salt. Remove to plate.

3. Add onion to skillet; cook and stir about 5 minutes or until translucent. Remove to plate.

4. Heat remaining 1 tablespoon oil in same skillet. Place 1 tortilla in skillet; top with one quarter of chicken, onion and cheese. Place second tortilla over filling; press down lightly. Cook quesadilla about 2 minutes per side or until browned and crisp. Repeat with remaining tortillas and filling.

5. Cut into wedges; serve with desired toppings.

NOTE: Be creative and use your own favorite fillings!

SHRIMP TAPAS IN SHERRY SAUCE

MAKES 4 SERVINGS

1 slice thick-cut bacon, cut crosswise into ¼-inch strips

2 ounces cremini or button mushrooms, cut into quarters

½ pound large raw shrimp (about 16), peeled and deveined (with tails on)

2 cloves garlic, thinly sliced

2 tablespoons medium dry sherry

1 tablespoon fresh lemon juice

¼ teaspoon red pepper flakes

1. Cook bacon in large skillet over medium heat until crisp. Remove from skillet with slotted spoon; drain on paper towels. Set aside.

2. Add mushrooms to bacon drippings; cook and stir 2 minutes. Add shrimp and garlic; cook and stir 3 minutes or until shrimp turn pink and opaque. Stir in sherry, lemon juice and red pepper flakes. Remove shrimp to serving bowl with slotted spoon.

3. Cook sauce 1 minute or until reduced and thickened. Pour over shrimp. Sprinkle with bacon.

CHICKEN NUGGETS WITH SPICY TOMATO DIPPING SAUCE

MAKES 4 SERVINGS

Spicy Tomato Dipping
Sauce (recipe follows)

½ cup panko bread crumbs

½ cup grated Parmesan
cheese

1 package (3 ounces)
ramen noodles, any
flavor, finely crushed*

1 teaspoon garlic powder

1 teaspoon dried basil

½ teaspoon salt

¼ teaspoon black pepper

1 egg, lightly beaten

1½ pounds boneless skinless
chicken breasts, cut
into 2½×1-inch pieces

½ cup vegetable oil

Discard seasoning packet.

1. Prepare Spicy Tomato Dipping Sauce; set aside. Combine panko, cheese, noodles, garlic powder, basil, salt and pepper in large bowl. Place egg in shallow dish. Dip chicken in egg; shake off excess. Coat with panko mixture.

2. Heat oil in large skillet over medium heat. Cook chicken in batches about 5 minutes or until cooked through, turning once. Serve with Spicy Tomato Dipping Sauce.

SPICY TOMATO DIPPING SAUCE

MAKES 1½ CUPS

1 tablespoon olive oil

1 small onion, chopped

2 cloves garlic, minced

¼ teaspoon ground red pepper

1 can (about 14 ounces) fire-roasted diced tomatoes

1. Heat oil in medium skillet. Add onion and garlic; cook and stir about 3 minutes or until onion is tender and golden brown. Stir in ground red pepper.

2. Remove skillet from heat; add tomatoes. Process in blender or food processor until smooth. Return to skillet and cook about 10 minutes or until thickened and reduced to 1½ cups.

SPICY BBQ PARTY FRANKS

MAKES 6 TO 8 SERVINGS

1 tablespoon butter

1 package (1 pound) cocktail franks

⅓ cup cola

⅓ cup ketchup

2 tablespoons hot pepper sauce

2 tablespoons packed dark brown sugar

1 tablespoon cider vinegar

1. Melt butter in medium skillet over medium heat. Pierce cocktail franks with fork. Add franks to skillet; cook until slightly browned.

2. Stir in cola, ketchup, hot pepper sauce, brown sugar and vinegar. Reduce heat to low; cook until sauce is reduced to sticky glaze.

MASHED POTATO CAKES

MAKES 4 SERVINGS

- 2 cups cold mashed potatoes
- ⅓ cup shredded Cheddar cheese
- 3 slices bacon, crisp-cooked and crumbled
- 2 egg yolks, beaten
- 2 tablespoons chopped fresh parsley
- 2 tablespoons snipped fresh chives
- 1 tablespoon all-purpose flour
- 1 teaspoon salt
- ⅛ teaspoon black pepper
- 3 tablespoons vegetable oil

1. Combine mashed potatoes, cheese, bacon, egg yolks, parsley, chives, flour, salt and pepper in large bowl, mix well.

2. Heat oil in large skillet over medium heat. Scoop ¼ cupfuls of potato mixture into skillet. Cook 8 to 10 minutes per side or until golden brown.

ELEGANT SHRIMP SCAMPI

MAKES 8 SERVINGS

¼ cup (½ stick) plus
   2 tablespoons butter

6 to 8 cloves garlic, minced

1½ pounds large raw shrimp
   (about 16), peeled and
   deveined (with tails on)

6 green onions, thinly
   sliced

¼ cup dry white wine

Juice of 1 lemon (about
   2 tablespoons)

¼ cup chopped fresh
   parsley

Salt and black pepper

Lemon slices (optional)

1. Clarify butter by melting it in small saucepan over low heat. *Do not stir.* Skim off white foam that forms on top. Strain clarified butter through cheesecloth into glass measuring cup to yield ⅓ cup. Discard cheesecloth and milky residue at bottom of pan.

2. Heat clarified butter in large skillet over medium heat. Add garlic; cook and stir 1 to 2 minutes or until softened but not browned.

3. Add shrimp, green onions, wine and lemon juice; cook and stir 3 to 4 minutes or until shrimp are pink and opaque. *Do not overcook.*

4. Stir in parsley and season with salt and pepper. Garnish with lemon slices.

QUESADILLA GRANDE

MAKES 1 SERVING

2 (8-inch) flour tortillas

2 to 3 large fresh stemmed spinach leaves

2 to 3 slices (about 3 ounces) cooked boneless skinless chicken breast

2 tablespoons salsa

1 tablespoon chopped fresh cilantro

¼ cup (1 ounce) shredded Monterey Jack cheese

2 teaspoons butter or margarine (optional)

1. Place 1 tortilla in large nonstick skillet; cover tortilla with spinach leaves. Place chicken in single layer over spinach. Spoon salsa over chicken. Sprinkle with cilantro; top with cheese. Place remaining tortilla on top, pressing tortilla down so filling becomes compact.

2. Cook over medium heat 4 to 5 minutes or until bottom tortilla is lightly browned. Holding top tortilla in place, gently turn over. Continue cooking 4 minutes or until bottom tortilla is browned and cheese is melted. For a crispy finish, place butter in skillet to melt; lift quesadilla to let butter flow into center of skillet. Cook 30 seconds. Turn over; continue cooking 30 seconds. Cut in half to serve.

BEER BATTER TEMPURA

MAKES 4 SERVINGS

1½ cups all-purpose flour

1½ cups Japanese beer, chilled

1 teaspoon salt

Dipping Sauce (recipe follows)

Vegetable oil for frying

½ pound green beans or asparagus tips

1 large sweet potato, cut into ¼-inch slices

1 medium eggplant, cut into ¼-inch slices

1. Combine flour, beer and salt in medium bowl just until mixed. Batter should be thin and lumpy. *Do not overmix.* Let stand 15 minutes. Meanwhile, prepare Dipping Sauce.

2. Heat 1 inch oil in large skillet to 375°F; adjust heat to maintain temperature.

3. Dip 10 to 12 green beans in batter; add to hot oil. Fry until light golden brown. Remove to wire racks or paper towels to drain; keep warm. Repeat with remaining vegetables, working with only one vegetable at a time and being careful not to crowd vegetables. Serve with Dipping Sauce.

DIPPING SAUCE

MAKES ABOUT 1 CUP

½ cup soy sauce

2 tablespoons rice wine

1 tablespoon sugar

½ teaspoon white vinegar

2 teaspoons minced fresh ginger

1 clove garlic, minced

2 green onions, thinly sliced

Combine soy sauce, rice wine, sugar and vinegar in small saucepan; cook and stir over medium heat 3 minutes or until sugar dissolves. Add ginger and garlic; cook and stir 2 minutes. Stir in green onions; remove from heat.

MINI BEEF ALBÓNDIGAS

MAKES 12 SERVINGS

1 pound Ground Beef

¼ cup soft whole wheat bread crumbs

1 large egg, slightly beaten

4 tablespoons chopped fresh cilantro, divided

1 teaspoon ground chipotle chili powder, divided

½ teaspoon salt

1 can (15 ounces) tomato sauce

2 tablespoons water

Chopped fresh cilantro (optional)

1. Combine Ground Beef, bread crumbs, egg, 2 tablespoons cilantro, ½ teaspoon chipotle chili powder and salt in large bowl, mixing lightly but thoroughly. Shape into 24 one-inch meatballs. Heat large nonstick skillet over medium heat until hot. Place meatballs in skillet; cook 8 minutes or until browned on all sides.

2. Add tomato sauce, remaining 2 tablespoons cilantro, water and remaining ½ teaspoon chipotle chili powder; bring to a boil. Reduce heat. Cover; simmer 8 to 10 minutes, stirring once.

3. Serve meatballs on skewers or on platter with toothpicks. Sprinkle with cilantro, if desired.

Courtesy The Beef Checkoff

SOUPS, STEWS AND CHILIES

LONG SOUP

MAKES 4 SERVINGS

1½ tablespoons vegetable oil

¼ small head cabbage, shredded

8 ounces boneless lean pork, cut into thin strips

6 cups chicken broth

2 tablespoons soy sauce

½ teaspoon minced fresh ginger

8 green onions, cut diagonally into ½-inch slices

4 ounces uncooked Chinese-style thin egg noodles

1. Heat oil in large skillet over medium-high heat. Add cabbage and pork; cook and stir 5 minutes or until pork is no longer pink in center.

2. Add broth, soy sauce and ginger. Bring to a boil. Reduce heat to low; simmer 10 minutes, stirring occasionally. Stir in green onions.

3. Add noodles; cook 2 to 4 minutes or until noodles are tender.

FRESH TOMATO CHILI

MAKES 4 SERVINGS

1 tablespoon olive oil

1 small onion, chopped (about 1 cup)

1 clove garlic, minced

1 medium tomato, diced (about 1½ cups)

1 cup frozen corn

1 cup canned kidney beans, rinsed and drained

1 can (8 ounces) tomato sauce

½ to ⅔ cup chicken or vegetable broth, divided

1 teaspoon chili powder

½ teaspoon ground cumin

¼ teaspoon dried oregano

⅛ teaspoon salt

⅛ teaspoon black pepper

⅛ teaspoon red pepper flakes

Hot cooked brown rice

1. Heat oil in large nonstick skillet over medium-high heat. Add onion and garlic; cook and stir 5 minutes. Add tomato and corn; cook and stir 2 minutes.

2. Add beans, tomato sauce, ½ cup broth, chili powder, cumin, oregano, salt, black pepper and red pepper flakes. Simmer 6 to 8 minutes. Add remaining broth if chili is too thick. Top each serving with rice.

FRENCH LENTIL SOUP

MAKES 4 TO 6 SERVINGS

3 tablespoons olive oil

1 medium onion, chopped

1 carrot, chopped

1 stalk celery, chopped

1 clove garlic, minced

½ pound dried lentils, rinsed and sorted

3 cups chicken broth

1 can (about 14 ounces) stewed tomatoes

½ cup cola

Salt and black pepper

½ cup grated Parmesan cheese (optional)

1. Heat oil in large skillet over medium heat. Add onion, carrot, celery and garlic; cook 9 minutes or until vegetables are tender but not browned, stirring occasionally.

2. Stir in lentils, broth, tomatoes and cola; bring to a boil over high heat. Reduce heat to low; cover and simmer 30 minutes or lentils are until tender.

3. Season with salt and pepper; sprinkle with Parmesan, if desired.

BEEF SOUP WITH NOODLES

MAKES 4 SERVINGS

2 tablespoons soy sauce

1 teaspoon minced fresh ginger

¼ teaspoon red pepper flakes

1 boneless beef top sirloin steak (about ¾ pound)

1 tablespoon peanut or vegetable oil

2 cups sliced fresh mushrooms

2 cans (about 14 ounces each) beef broth

1 cup (3 ounces) fresh snow peas, cut diagonally into 1-inch pieces

1½ cups hot cooked egg noodles (2 ounces uncooked)

1 green onion, cut diagonally into thin slices

1 teaspoon dark sesame oil (optional)

Red bell pepper strips (optional)

1. Combine soy sauce, ginger and red pepper flakes in small bowl. Pour mixture evenly over both sides of steak. Marinate 15 minutes.

2. Heat peanut oil in deep skillet over medium-high heat. Drain steak; reserve marinade (there will only be a small amount of marinade). Add steak to skillet; cook 5 minutes per side or until desired doneness. Remove to large cutting board; let stand 10 minutes to cool slightly.

3. Meanwhile, add mushrooms to skillet; stir-fry 2 minutes. Add broth, snow peas and reserved marinade; bring to a boil, scraping up any browned bits from bottom of skillet. Reduce heat to medium-low. Stir in noodles.

4. Cut steak lengthwise in half, then crosswise into thin slices. Stir into soup; heat through. Stir in green onion and sesame oil, if desired. Ladle soup into bowls; garnish with bell pepper strips.

TORTILLA SOUP

MAKES 4 SERVINGS

Vegetable oil

3 (6- or 7-inch) corn tortillas, halved and cut into strips

½ cup chopped onion

1 clove garlic, minced

2 cans (about 14 ounces each) chicken broth

1 can (about 14 ounces) diced tomatoes

1 cup shredded cooked chicken

2 teaspoons fresh lime juice

1 small avocado, diced

2 tablespoons chopped fresh cilantro

1. Pour oil to depth of ½ inch in large skillet. Heat over medium-high heat until oil reaches 360°F on deep-fry thermometer. Add tortilla strips, a few at a time; fry 1 minute or until crisp and lightly browned. Remove with slotted spoon; drain on paper towels. Drain and wipe skillet clean with paper towels.

2. Heat 2 teaspoons oil in same skillet over medium heat. Add onion and garlic; cook and stir 6 to 8 minutes or until onion is soft. Add broth and tomatoes; bring to a boil. Cover; reduce heat and simmer 15 minutes.

3. Add chicken and lime juice; simmer 5 minutes. Top soup with tortilla strips, avocado and cilantro.

CHILI

MAKES 6 TO 8 SERVINGS

2 pounds ground beef

2 cups finely chopped white onions

1 to 2 dried de arbol chiles

2 cloves garlic, minced

1 teaspoon ground cumin

½ to 1 teaspoon salt

¼ teaspoon ground cloves

1 can (28 ounces) whole tomatoes, undrained and coarsely chopped

½ cup orange juice

½ cup tequila or water

¼ cup tomato paste

1 tablespoon grated orange peel

Lime wedges and sprigs fresh cilantro (optional)

1. Brown beef in large skillet over medium-high heat 6 to 8 minutes, stirring to break up meat. Drain fat. Reduce heat to medium. Add onions; cook and stir 5 minutes or until tender.

2. Crush chiles into fine flakes in mortar with pestle. Add chiles, garlic, cumin, salt and cloves to skillet; cook and stir 30 seconds.

3. Stir in tomatoes with juice, orange juice, tequila, tomato paste and orange peel. Bring to a boil over high heat. Reduce heat to low. Cover and simmer 1½ hours, stirring occasionally.

4. Uncover skillet. Cook and stir chili over medium-low heat 10 to 15 minutes or until thickened slightly. Ladle into bowls. Garnish with lime wedges and cilantro.

VEGGIE BEEF SKILLET SOUP

MAKES 4 SERVINGS

¾ pound ground beef

1 tablespoon olive oil

2 cups coarsely chopped cabbage

1 cup chopped green bell pepper

2 cups water

1 can (about 14 ounces) stewed tomatoes

1 cup frozen mixed vegetables

⅓ cup ketchup

1 tablespoon beef bouillon granules

2 teaspoons Worcestershire sauce

2 teaspoons balsamic vinegar

⅛ teaspoon red pepper flakes

¼ cup chopped fresh parsley

1. Brown beef in large skillet over medium-high heat 6 to 8 minutes, stirring to break up meat. Drain fat. Transfer to plate.

2. Heat oil in same skillet. Add cabbage and bell pepper; cook and stir 4 minutes or until cabbage is wilted. Add beef, water, tomatoes, mixed vegetables, ketchup, bouillon, Worcestershire sauce, vinegar and red pepper flakes; bring to a boil. Reduce heat; cover and simmer 20 minutes.

3. Remove from heat; let stand 5 minutes. Stir in parsley just before serving.

SPICY THAI SHRIMP SOUP

MAKES 8 SERVINGS

1 tablespoon vegetable oil

1 pound medium raw shrimp, peeled and deveined, shells reserved

1 jalapeño pepper,* cut into slivers

1 tablespoon paprika

¼ teaspoon ground red pepper

4 cans (about 14 ounces each) chicken broth

1 (½-inch) strip *each* lemon and lime peel

1 can (15 ounces) straw mushrooms, drained

Juice of 1 lemon

Juice of 1 lime

2 tablespoons soy sauce

1 red Thai pepper* or red jalapeño pepper* *or* ¼ small red bell pepper, cut into strips

¼ cup fresh cilantro leaves

Chile peppers can sting and irritate the skin, so wear rubber gloves when handling peppers and do not touch your eyes.

1. Heat large skillet over medium-high heat 1 minute. Add oil; heat 30 seconds. Add shrimp and jalapeño pepper; stir-fry 1 minute. Add paprika and ground red pepper; stir-fry 1 minute or until shrimp are pink and opaque. Transfer shrimp mixture to medium bowl.

2. Add shrimp shells to skillet; cook and stir 30 seconds. Add broth and lemon and lime peels; bring to a boil. Reduce heat to low; cover and simmer 15 minutes.

3. Remove and discard shells and peels with slotted spoon. Add mushrooms and shrimp mixture to broth; bring to a boil over medium heat. Stir in lemon and lime juices, soy sauce and Thai pepper; cook until heated through. Ladle soup into bowls. Sprinkle with cilantro. Serve immediately.

BEEF CHILI FIVE WAYS

MAKES 4 SERVINGS

1 pound Ground Beef (93% lean or leaner)

1 can (15½ ounces) black beans, rinsed and drained

1 can (14 to 14½-ounces) reduced-sodium or regular beef broth

1 can (14½ ounces) diced tomatoes with green chiles

2 tablespoons chili powder

TOPPINGS:
Shredded Cheddar cheese, chopped fresh cilantro, minced green onion (optional)

1. Heat large nonstick skillet over medium heat until hot. Add Ground Beef; cook 8 to 10 minutes, breaking into ¾-inch crumbles and stirring occasionally. Pour off drippings.

2. Stir in beans, broth, tomatoes and chili powder; bring to a boil. Reduce heat. Cover and simmer 20 minutes to develop flavors, stirring occasionally. Garnish with Toppings, as desired.

MOROCCAN VARIATION: Prepare recipe as directed above, adding ¼ teaspoon pumpkin pie spice and ¼ cup chopped pitted dates or golden raisins with ingredients in step 2. Serve over hot cooked couscous. Garnish with toasted sliced almonds, chopped fresh mint and Greek yogurt, as desired.

MEXICAN VARIATION: Prepare recipe as directed above, adding 1 tablespoon cocoa powder with ingredients in step 2. Garnish with chopped fresh cilantro, pepitas (pumpkin seeds) and corn tortilla chips, as desired. Serve with corn tortillas.

ITALIAN VARIATION: Prepare recipe as directed above, adding 1½ teaspoons fennel seed with ingredients in step 2. Before removing from heat, stir in 3 cups fresh baby spinach. Cover; turn off heat and let stand 3 to 5 minutes or until spinach is just wilted. Serve over hot cooked orecchiette or cavatappi, if desired. Garnish with grated Parmesan cheese and pine nuts, as desired.

CINCINNATI VARIATION: Prepare recipe as directed above, adding 3 tablespoons white vinegar and 1 teaspoon ground cinnamon with ingredients in step 2. Serve over hot cooked elbow macaroni. Garnish with chopped white onion, sour cream and shredded Cheddar cheese, as desired.

COOK'S TIPS: Cooking times are for fresh or thoroughly thawed Ground Beef. Ground Beef should be cooked to an internal temperature of 160°F. Color is not a reliable indicator of Ground Beef doneness.

For a thicker consistency, prepare as directed, adding 1 tablespoon cornmeal with ingredients in step 2.

Courtesy The Beef Checkoff

SKILLET CHICKEN SOUP

MAKES 6 SERVINGS

1 teaspoon paprika

½ teaspoon salt

¼ teaspoon black pepper

¾ pound boneless skinless chicken breasts or thighs, cut into ¾-inch pieces

2 teaspoons vegetable oil

1 large onion, chopped

1 red bell pepper, cut into ½-inch pieces

3 cloves garlic, minced

3 cups chicken broth

1 can (19 ounces) cannellini beans or small white beans, rinsed and drained

3 cups sliced savoy or napa cabbage

½ cup herb-flavored croutons, slightly crushed (optional)

1. Combine paprika, salt and black pepper in medium bowl; stir to blend. Add chicken; toss to coat.

2. Heat oil in large deep nonstick skillet over medium-high heat. Add chicken, onion, bell pepper and garlic; cook and stir 8 minutes or until chicken is cooked through.

3. Add broth and beans; bring to a simmer. Cover and simmer 5 minutes. Stir in cabbage; cover and simmer 3 minutes or until cabbage is wilted. Ladle into six shallow bowls; top evenly with crushed croutons, if desired.

TIP: Savoy cabbage, also called curly cabbage, is round with pale green crinkled leaves. Napa cabbage is also known as Chinese cabbage and is elongated with light green stalks.

WHITE BEAN CHILI

MAKES 6 SERVINGS

Nonstick cooking spray

1 pound ground chicken

3 cups coarsely chopped celery

1½ cups coarsely chopped onions (about 2 medium)

3 cloves garlic, minced

4 teaspoons chili powder

1½ teaspoons ground cumin

¾ teaspoon ground allspice

¾ teaspoon ground cinnamon

½ teaspoon black pepper

1 can (16 ounces) whole tomatoes, undrained and coarsely chopped

1 can (about 15 ounces) Great Northern beans, rinsed and drained

2 cups chicken broth

1. Spray large nonstick skillet with cooking spray; heat over medium heat. Add chicken; cook and stir until browned, breaking into pieces. Remove chicken; drain fat from skillet.

2. Add celery, onions and garlic to skillet; cook and stir over medium heat 5 to 7 minutes or until tender. Sprinkle with chili powder, cumin, allspice, cinnamon and pepper; cook and stir 1 minute.

3. Return chicken to skillet. Stir in tomatoes with juice, beans and broth; bring to a boil. Reduce heat to low. Simmer, uncovered, 15 minutes.

CALYPSO BEEF SOUP

MAKES 6 SERVINGS

1½ pounds Ground Beef (95% lean)

1 cup diced peeled sweet potato

½ cup chopped onion

½ cup chopped red bell pepper

1 teaspoon curry powder

2 tablespoons all-purpose flour

2 cups water or ready-to-serve beef broth

1 can (15½ ounces) black-eyed peas, rinsed, drained

1 can (13½ ounces) light unsweetened coconut milk

2 cups packed fresh baby spinach leaves

3 tablespoons chopped fresh thyme

Salt and ground black pepper

1. Heat large nonstick skillet over medium heat until hot. Add Ground Beef; cook 8 to 10 minutes, breaking into ¾-inch crumbles and stirring occasionally. Remove from skillet with slotted spoon. Pour off drippings in pan; add sweet potato, onion, bell pepper and curry powder. Cook 4 to 5 minutes or until onion and pepper are crisp-tender, stirring occasionally. Stir in flour; cook and stir 1 minute.

2. Return beef to skillet. Stir in water, black-eyed peas and coconut milk; bring to a boil. Reduce heat; cover and simmer 5 to 8 minutes or until sweet potato is tender. Stir in spinach and thyme. Cook 1 minute or until spinach wilts. Season with salt and black pepper, as desired.

Courtesy The Beef Checkoff

RED & GREEN NO-BEAN CHILI

MAKES 10 TO 12 SERVINGS

4 pounds ground beef

2 large onions, chopped

3 banana peppers, seeded and sliced

¼ cup chili powder

2 tablespoons minced garlic

1 can (about 28 ounces) diced tomatoes with mild green chiles, undrained

1 can (about 14 ounces) beef broth

2 cans (4 ounces each) diced mild green chiles, drained

2 tablespoons ground cumin

2 tablespoons cider or malt vinegar

1 to 2 tablespoons hot paprika

1 tablespoon dried oregano

Hot pepper sauce

Diced avocado and red bell pepper (optional)

1. Brown beef in large skillet over medium-high heat 6 to 8 minutes, stirring to break up meat. Drain fat. Stir in onions, banana peppers, chili powder and garlic. Reduce heat to medium-low; cook 30 minutes, stirring occasionally.

2. Add tomatoes with juice, broth, green chiles, cumin, vinegar, paprika, oregano and hot pepper sauce; cook and stir 30 minutes. Garnish with avocado and red bell pepper.

CARIBBEAN CALLALOO SOUP

MAKES 6 SERVINGS

1 teaspoon olive oil

1 large onion, chopped

4 cloves garlic, minced

¾ pound boneless skinless chicken breasts, thinly sliced crosswise

1½ pounds butternut squash, cut into ½-inch cubes

3 cans (about 14 ounces each) chicken broth

2 jalapeño peppers,* seeded and minced

2 teaspoons dried thyme

½ (10-ounce) package fresh spinach, stemmed and torn

¼ cup plus 2 tablespoons shredded sweetened coconut**

Jalapeño peppers can sting and irritate the skin, so wear rubber gloves when handling peppers and do not touch your eyes.

**To toast coconut, spread in a single layer in heavy-bottomed skillet. Cook and stir 1 to 2 minutes or until lightly browned. Remove from skillet immediately.*

1. Heat oil in large nonstick skillet over medium-low heat. Add onion and garlic; cook and stir 5 minutes or until onion is tender. Add chicken; cover and cook 5 to 7 minutes or until chicken is no longer pink in center.

2. Add squash, broth, jalapeño peppers and thyme; bring to a boil over medium-high heat. Reduce heat to low. Simmer, covered, 15 to 20 minutes or until squash is very tender.

3. Remove skillet from heat; stir in spinach until wilted. Ladle into bowls and sprinkle with toasted coconut.

CHILI Á LA MEXICO

2 pounds ground beef

2 cups finely chopped onions

2 cloves garlic, minced

1 can (28 ounces) whole tomatoes, undrained and coarsely chopped

1 can (6 ounces) tomato paste

1½ to 2 tablespoons chili powder

1 teaspoon ground cumin

¼ teaspoon salt

¼ teaspoon ground red pepper

¼ teaspoon ground cloves (optional)

Lime wedges and sprigs fresh cilantro (optional)

1. Brown beef in large skillet over medium-high heat 6 to 8 minutes, stirring to break up meat. Drain fat. Add onions and garlic; cook and stir 5 minutes or until onions are softened.

2. Stir in tomatoes with juice, tomato paste, chili powder, cumin, salt, ground red pepper and cloves, if desired. Bring to a boil over high heat. Reduce heat to low; cover and simmer 30 minutes, stirring occasionally. Ladle into bowls. Garnish with lime wedges and cilantro, if desired.

SKILLET SUPPERS

EASY CHICKEN PARMESAN

MAKES 4 SERVINGS

1 tablespoon olive oil

4 boneless skinless chicken breasts

1 medium onion, chopped

1 small zucchini, sliced

1 jar (26 ounces) pasta sauce

½ teaspoon dried basil

½ teaspoon dried oregano

8 ounces fresh mozzarella cheese, cut into thin slices

¼ cup grated Parmesan cheese

Hot cooked spaghetti

1. Preheat broiler.

2. Heat oil in large skillet over medium-high heat. Add chicken; cook 5 to 7 minutes or until browned on both sides. Add onion and zucchini; cook 5 minutes or until vegetables are softened. Stir in pasta sauce, basil and oregano. Top chicken with mozzarella slices.

3. Broil 6 inches from heat 5 to 7 minutes or until chicken is no longer pink in center and cheese is beginning to brown. Sprinkle each serving with Parmesan cheese and serve over spaghetti.

CLASSIC PATTY MELTS

MAKES 4 SERVINGS

5 tablespoons butter, divided

2 large yellow onions, thinly sliced

¾ teaspoon plus pinch of salt, divided

1 pound ground chuck (80% lean)

½ teaspoon garlic powder

½ teaspoon onion powder

¼ teaspoon black pepper

8 slices marble rye bread

½ cup Thousand Island dressing

8 slices deli American or Swiss cheese

1. Melt 2 tablespoons butter in large skillet over medium heat. Add onions and pinch of salt; cook 20 minutes or until onions are very soft and golden brown, stirring occasionally. Remove to small bowl; wipe out skillet with paper towel.

2. Combine beef, remaining ¾ teaspoon salt, garlic powder, onion powder and pepper in medium bowl; mix gently. Shape into four patties about the size and shape of bread slices and ¼ to ½ inch thick.

3. Melt 1 tablespoon butter in same skillet over medium-high heat. Add patties, two at a time; cook 3 minutes or until bottoms are browned, pressing down gently to form crust. Turn patties; cook 3 minutes or until browned. Remove patties to plate; wipe out skillet with paper towel.

4. Spread one side of each bread slice with dressing. Top 4 bread slices with cheese slice, patty, caramelized onions, another cheese slice and remaining bread slices.

5. Melt 1 tablespoon butter in same skillet over medium heat. Add two sandwiches to skillet; cook 4 minutes or until golden brown, pressing down to crisp bread. Turn sandwiches and cook 4 minutes or until golden brown and cheese is melted. Repeat with remaining sandwiches and 1 tablespoon butter.

PUMPKIN CURRY

MAKES 4 SERVINGS

1 tablespoon vegetable oil

1 package (14 ounces) extra firm tofu, drained and cut into 1-inch cubes

¼ cup Thai red curry paste

2 cloves garlic, minced

1 can (15 ounces) solid-pack pumpkin

1 can (14 ounces) coconut milk

1 cup water

1½ teaspoons salt

1 teaspoon sriracha sauce

4 cups cut-up fresh vegetables (broccoli, cauliflower, red bell pepper and/or sweet potato)

½ cup peas

2 cups hot cooked rice

¼ cup shredded fresh basil (optional)

1. Heat oil in large skillet over high heat. Add tofu; cook and stir 2 to 3 minutes or until lightly browned. Add curry paste and garlic; cook and stir 1 minute or until tofu is coated. Add pumpkin, coconut milk, water, salt and sriracha; bring to a boil. Stir in vegetables.

2. Reduce heat to medium; cover and simmer 20 minutes or until vegetables are tender. Stir in peas; cook 1 minute or until heated through. Serve over rice; top with basil, if desired.

MEXICAN MONGOLIAN BEEF

MAKES 4 SERVINGS

⅓ cup ORTEGA® Taco Sauce, any variety

⅓ cup hoisin sauce

1 teaspoon ground ginger

1 pound sirloin steak

1 tablespoon cornstarch

2 tablespoons olive oil

1 large onion, sliced

1 to 2 cups cooked vegetables, such as carrots, broccoli or green beans (optional)

Hot cooked rice

4 green onions, sliced

1 tablespoon sesame seeds

COMBINE taco sauce, hoisin sauce and ginger in small bowl; mix well. Set aside.

CUT steak diagonally against the grain into thin slices. Place in medium bowl; toss with cornstarch until evenly coated.

HEAT oil in large skillet over medium heat until hot. Add onion; cook and stir 3 to 4 minutes or until onion is translucent.

ADD steak; cook and stir 5 minutes or until meat is browned. Add sauce mixture and vegetables, if desired; cook and stir 2 minutes or until heated through.

SERVE over rice. Top evenly with green onions and sesame seeds.

TIP: For more savory flavor, mix any variety of ORTEGA® Original Salsa into the cooked rice before serving with the dish.

PORK CHOPS WITH BELL PEPPERS AND SWEET POTATO

MAKES 4 SERVINGS

4 pork loin chops (about 1 pound), cut about ½ inch thick

1 teaspoon lemon-pepper seasoning

Nonstick cooking spray

½ cup water

1 tablespoon lemon juice

1 teaspoon dried fines herbes, crushed

½ teaspoon beef bouillon granules

1¼ cups red or yellow bell pepper strips or a combination

1 cup sliced sweet potato, cut into 1-inch pieces

¾ cup sliced onion

4 cups hot cooked rice (optional)

1. Trim fat from chops; discard. Rub both sides of chops with lemon-pepper seasoning. Coat large skillet with cooking spray. Heat skillet over medium-high heat. Add chops; cook 5 minutes or until browned on both sides.

2. Combine water, lemon juice, fines herbes and bouillon granules in small bowl; stir to blend. Pour over chops. Reduce heat to medium-low. Cover; simmer 5 minutes.

3. Add bell pepper, sweet potato and onion to skillet; return to a boil. Reduce heat. Cover; simmer 10 to 15 minutes or until chops are slightly pink in center and vegetables are crisp-tender. Remove chops and vegetables from skillet; keep warm.

4. Bring remaining juices in skillet to a boil over high heat. Reduce heat to medium. Cook and stir 6 to 8 minutes or until mixture slightly thickens, stirring occasionally. Arrange chops and vegetables on large serving plate; spoon sauce over chops and vegetables. Serve with rice, if desired.

SKILLET LASAGNA WITH VEGETABLES

MAKES 6 SERVINGS

½ pound hot Italian turkey sausage, casings removed

½ pound ground turkey

2 stalks celery, sliced

⅓ cup chopped onion

2 cups marinara sauce

1⅓ cups water

4 ounces uncooked bowtie (farfalle) pasta

1 medium zucchini, halved lengthwise and cut into ½-inch-thick slices (2 cups)

¾ cup chopped green or yellow bell pepper

½ cup (2 ounces) shredded mozzarella cheese

½ cup ricotta cheese

2 tablespoons finely grated Parmesan cheese

1. Heat large skillet over medium-high heat. Add sausage, ground turkey, celery and onion; cook and stir 6 to 8 minutes or until turkey is no longer pink. Stir in marinara sauce and water. Bring to a boil. Add pasta; stir. Reduce heat to medium-low; cover and simmer 12 minutes.

2. Stir in zucchini and bell pepper; cover and simmer 2 minutes. Uncover and simmer 4 to 6 minutes or until vegetables are crisp-tender.

3. Sprinkle with mozzarella. Combine ricotta and Parmesan cheeses in small bowl. Drop by rounded teaspoonfuls on top of mixture in skillet. Remove from heat; cover and let stand 10 minutes.

GRILLED ITALIAN CHICKEN PANINI

MAKES 6 SANDWICHES

6 small portobello mushroom caps (about 6 ounces)

½ cup plus 2 tablespoons balsamic vinaigrette dressing

1 loaf (16 ounces) Italian bread, cut into 12 slices

12 slices provolone cheese

1½ cups chopped cooked chicken

1 jar (12 ounces) roasted red peppers, drained

1. Brush mushrooms with 2 tablespoons dressing. Cook mushrooms in large nonstick skillet over medium-high heat 5 to 7 minutes or until soft. Cut diagonally into ½-inch slices.

2. For each sandwich, top 1 bread slice with 1 cheese slice, ¼ cup chicken, mushrooms, roasted red peppers, another cheese slice and another bread slice. Brush outsides of sandwiches with remaining dressing.

3. Heat large skillet over medium heat. Add sandwiches; place a clean heavy pan on top of sandwiches to weigh them down while cooking. Cook 4 to 6 minutes or until cheese is melted and bread is golden, turning once during cooking.

TIP: A rotisserie chicken will yield just enough chopped chicken for this recipe.

BEEF FAJITAS

MAKES 4 SERVINGS

1 teaspoon ground cumin

1 teaspoon dried oregano

¾ pound well-trimmed boneless beef top sirloin steak (about ¾ inch thick)

2 bell peppers (red, yellow, green or a combination), cut thinly into 1-inch strips

½ cup thinly sliced yellow or red onion

4 cloves garlic, minced

Nonstick cooking spray

½ cup jalapeño-flavored salsa

4 (7-inch) whole wheat flour tortillas, warmed

¼ cup chopped fresh cilantro

1. Rub cumin and oregano over both sides of steak. Heat large skillet over medium heat. Add steak; cook 3 to 4 minutes per side for medium-rare doneness. Transfer steak to large cutting board; tent with foil and let stand.

2. Add bell peppers, onion and garlic to same skillet. Coat vegetables with cooking spray; cook and stir 4 to 5 minutes or until crisp-tender. Add salsa; simmer 3 minutes.

3. Carve steak into thin slices and return to skillet. Toss well and heat through, about 1 minute. Spoon mixture down center of tortillas; top with cilantro and fold in half.

TIP: Tenting with foil is a way to allow grilled meat to continue to cook, without overcooking, while you prepare the rest of a recipe. To tent: drape a large sheet of foil over cooked meat, fold the foil slightly and let it sit loosely over the meat.

SASSY CHICKEN & PEPPERS

MAKES 4 SERVINGS

1 tablespoon Mexican seasoning*

4 boneless skinless chicken breasts (about ¼ pound each)

1 tablespoon vegetable oil

1 red onion, sliced

1 medium red bell pepper, cut into thin strips

1 medium yellow or green bell pepper, cut into thin strips

½ cup chunky salsa or chipotle salsa

2 tablespoons lime juice

Lime wedges (optional)

*If Mexican seasoning is not available, substitute 1 teaspoon chili powder, ½ teaspoon ground cumin, ½ teaspoon salt and ⅛ teaspoon ground red pepper.

1. Sprinkle seasoning over both sides of chicken; set aside.

2. Heat oil in large nonstick skillet over medium heat. Add onion; cook 3 minutes, stirring occasionally.

3. Add bell peppers; cook 3 minutes, stirring occasionally. Stir salsa and lime juice into vegetables.

4. Push vegetables to edge of skillet. Add chicken to skillet. Cook 5 minutes; turn. Continue to cook 4 minutes or until chicken is no longer pink in center and vegetables are tender.

5. Serve chicken over vegetable mixture. Garnish with lime wedges.

SALSA BACON BURGERS WITH GUACAMOLE

MAKES 4 BURGERS

1 pound ground beef

1 packet (1.25 ounces) ORTEGA® Taco Seasoning Mix

¼ cup ORTEGA® Salsa, any variety

2 ripe avocados

1 packet (1 ounce) ORTEGA® Guacamole Seasoning Mix

4 hamburger buns

8 slices cooked bacon

COMBINE ground beef, taco seasoning mix and salsa in large mixing bowl. With clean hands, form meat mixture into 4 patties.

CUT avocados in half and remove pits. Scoop out avocado meat and smash in small bowl. Add guacamole seasoning mix. Set aside.

HEAT large skillet over medium heat; cook burgers 5 minutes. Flip burgers and continue to cook another 7 minutes.

PLACE burgers on bottom of buns. Top each burger with dollop of guacamole, 2 slices bacon and top bun.

TIP: Make burgers half the size to create great sliders.

VEGGIE-PACKED SPAGHETTI & MEATBALLS

MAKES 4 SERVINGS

- 4 ounces uncooked spaghetti or vermicelli
- ¾ pound lean ground turkey or beef
- 1 package (10 ounces) frozen chopped spinach, thawed and pressed dry
- ½ cup fresh whole wheat bread crumbs*
- 1 egg white
- 1 teaspoon onion powder
- 1 teaspoon garlic powder
- ½ teaspoon black pepper
  Nonstick cooking spray
- 2 cups pasta sauce
- 2 cups (5 ounces) small broccoli florets
- ½ cup packaged julienned carrots

To make fresh bread crumbs, tear 1 slice bread into pieces; process in food processor until coarse crumbs form.

1. Cook spaghetti according to package directions, omitting salt. Drain.

2. Meanwhile, combine turkey, spinach, bread crumbs, egg white, onion powder, garlic powder and pepper in medium bowl; mix well. Shape into 32 (½-inch) meatballs.

3. Spray large skillet with cooking spray; heat over medium heat. Add meatballs; cook 8 to 10 minutes, turning to brown all sides.

4. Add pasta sauce, broccoli and carrots to skillet. Cover; bring to a simmer over medium-low heat. Cook 8 to 10 minutes or vegetables are tender and sauce is heated through.

5. Spoon sauce and meatballs evenly over spaghetti.

PAN-FRIED CAJUN BASS

MAKES 4 SERVINGS

2 tablespoons all-purpose flour

1 to 1½ teaspoons Cajun or Caribbean jerk seasoning

1 egg white

2 teaspoons water

⅓ cup seasoned dry bread crumbs

2 tablespoons cornmeal

4 skinless striped bass, halibut or cod fillets (4 to 6 ounces each), thawed if frozen

1 teaspoon butter

1 teaspoon olive oil

Chopped fresh parsley (optional)

4 lemon wedges

1. Combine flour and seasoning in medium resealable food storage bag. Beat egg white and water in small bowl. Combine bread crumbs and cornmeal in separate small bowl.

2. Working one at a time, add fillet to bag; shake to coat evenly. Dip in egg white mixture, letting excess drip back into bowl. Roll in bread crumb mixture, pressing lightly to adhere. Repeat with remaining fillets.

3. Melt butter and oil in large nonstick skillet over medium heat. Add fillets; cook 4 to 5 minutes per side or until golden brown and fish is opaque in center and flakes easily when tested with fork.

4. Sprinkle parsley over fish, if desired. Serve with lemon wedges.

BLACKENED SHRIMP WITH TOMATOES

MAKES 4 SERVINGS

1½ teaspoons paprika

1 teaspoon Italian seasoning

½ teaspoon garlic powder

¼ teaspoon black pepper

½ pound (about 24) small raw shrimp, peeled (with tails on)

1 tablespoon canola oil

1½ cups halved grape tomatoes

½ cup sliced onion, separated into rings

Lime wedges (optional)

1. Combine paprika, Italian seasoning, garlic powder and pepper in small bowl; add to large resealable food storage bag. Add shrimp, seal bag and shake to coat.

2. Heat oil in large skillet over medium-high heat. Add shrimp; cook 4 minutes or until shrimp are pink and opaque, turning occasionally.

3. Add tomatoes and onion to skillet; cook 1 minute or until tomatoes are heated through and onion is softened. Serve with lime wedges, if desired.

EMERALD ISLE LAMB CHOPS

MAKES 4 TO 6 SERVINGS

2 tablespoons vegetable or olive oil, divided

2 tablespoons coarse Dijon mustard

1 tablespoon Irish whiskey

1 tablespoon minced fresh rosemary

2 teaspoons minced garlic

1½ pounds loin lamb chops (about 6 chops)

½ teaspoon salt

½ teaspoon black pepper

¾ cup dry white wine

2 tablespoons black currant jam

1 to 2 tablespoons butter, cut into small pieces

1. Combine 1 tablespoon oil, mustard, whiskey, rosemary and garlic in small bowl to form paste. Season lamb chops with salt and pepper; spread paste over both sides. Cover; marinate 30 minutes at room temperature or refrigerate 2 to 3 hours.

2. Heat remaining 1 tablespoon oil in large skillet over medium-high heat. Add lamb chops in single layer; cook 2 to 3 minutes per side or until desired doneness. Remove to large serving plate and keep warm.

3. Drain excess fat from skillet. Add wine; cook and stir about 5 minutes, scraping up any browned bits from bottom of skillet. Stir in jam until well blended. Remove from heat; stir in butter until melted. Serve sauce over lamb chops.

SPEEDY TACOS

MAKES 2 SERVINGS

4 ounces ground beef
  sirloin

¼ cup chopped onion

1 clove garlic, minced

⅓ cup tomato sauce

1 tablespoon taco
  seasoning mix

6 taco shells

¼ cup (2 ounces) shredded
  Cheddar cheese

½ cup shredded lettuce

⅓ cup chopped tomato

¼ cup chopped onion

  Hot pepper sauce
  (optional)

1. Heat small skillet over medium heat. Add beef, onion and garlic; cook and stir 5 minutes until beef is browned, breaking up meat with spoon. Add tomato sauce and taco seasoning mix; cook 5 minutes.

2. Warm taco shells in oven following package directions.

3. Fill taco shells with meat mixture, cheese, lettuce, tomato and onion. Serve with hot pepper sauce, if desired.

CRISPY BUTTERMILK FRIED CHICKEN

MAKES 4 SERVINGS

- 2 cups buttermilk
- 1 tablespoon hot pepper sauce
- 3 pounds bone-in chicken pieces
- 2 cups all-purpose flour
- 2 teaspoons salt
- 2 teaspoons poultry seasoning
- 1 teaspoon garlic salt
- 1 teaspoon paprika
- 1 teaspoon ground red pepper
- 1 teaspoon black pepper
- 1 cup vegetable oil

1. Combine buttermilk and hot pepper sauce in large resealable food storage bag. Add chicken; seal bag. Turn to coat. Refrigerate 2 hours or up to 24 hours.

2. Combine flour, salt, poultry seasoning, garlic salt, paprika, ground red pepper and black pepper in another large resealable food storage bag or shallow baking dish; mix well. Working in batches, remove chicken from buttermilk; shake off excess. Add to flour mixture; shake to coat.

3. Heat oil over medium heat in heavy deep skillet until deep-fry thermometer registers 350°F. Working in batches, fry chicken 30 minutes or until cooked through (165°F), turning occasionally to brown all sides. Drain on paper towels.

NOTE: Carefully monitor the temperature of the oil during cooking. It should not drop below 325°F or go higher than 350°F. Never leave hot oil unattended.

CHICKEN AND CHILE STIR-FRY

MAKES 4 SERVINGS

½ cup orange juice

4½ teaspoons oyster sauce

1 tablespoon minced fresh ginger

1 teaspoon cornstarch

Nonstick cooking spray

12 ounces boneless skinless chicken breasts, thinly sliced

4 ounces (about 6) jalapeño peppers,* stemmed, seeded and thinly sliced (½ cup)

4 ounces (about 3) poblano peppers, stemmed, seeded and thinly sliced (¾ cup)

8 cloves garlic, thinly sliced (2 tablespoons)

1 teaspoon olive oil

¼ cup slivered fresh basil or mint leaves

3 cups hot cooked rice

*Jalapeño and other peppers can sting and irritate the skin, so wear rubber gloves when handling peppers and do not touch your eyes.

1. Blend orange juice, oyster sauce and ginger into cornstarch in small bowl; set aside.

2. Spray large nonstick skillet with cooking spray; heat over medium-high heat. Add half the chicken; cook and stir 4 minutes or until chicken is no longer pink in center. Remove; set aside. Repeat with remaining chicken.

3. Add jalapeño peppers, poblano peppers, garlic and oil to same skillet; reduce heat to medium. Cook, partially covered, 8 minutes, stirring often, or until peppers are tender. (If skillet becomes dry and peppers stick, add 1 to 2 tablespoons water.) Return chicken to skillet. Add orange juice mixture; cook and stir until sauce boils and thickens slightly. Remove from heat; stir in basil. Serve over rice.

NOTE: To add a subtle smoky flavor, roast jalapeño and poblano peppers. When peppers are cool enough to handle, peel skin and slice.

GRILLED 3-CHEESE SANDWICHES

MAKES 2 SANDWICHES

2 slices (1 ounce each) Muenster cheese

2 slices (1 ounce each) Swiss cheese

2 slices (1 ounce each) Cheddar cheese

2 teaspoons Dijon mustard or Dijon mustard mayonnaise

4 slices sourdough bread

2 teaspoons melted butter

1. Place 1 slice of each cheese on 2 bread slices. Spread mustard over cheese; top with remaining bread slices. Brush outsides of sandwiches with butter.

2. Heat large skillet over medium heat. Add sandwiches; press down lightly with spatula or weigh down with small plate. Cook 4 minutes per side or until cheese is melted and sandwiches are golden brown.

SIZZLING SIDE DISHES

CASHEW GREEN BEANS

MAKES 4 SERVINGS

1 tablespoon peanut or vegetable oil

1 small onion, cut into thin wedges

2 cloves garlic, minced

1 package (10 ounces) frozen julienne-cut green beans, thawed, drained and patted dry

2 tablespoons oyster sauce

1 tablespoon rice vinegar

1 tablespoon honey

¼ cup coarsely chopped cashew nuts or peanuts

Heat oil in large skillet over medium-high heat. Add onion and garlic; cook and stir 3 minutes. Add green beans; cook and stir 2 minutes. Add oyster sauce, vinegar and honey; cook and stir 1 minute or until heated through. Remove from heat; stir in cashews.

CANTONESE RICE CAKE PATTIES

MAKES ABOUT 9 PATTIES

2 cups cooked rice, chilled

⅓ cup chopped red bell pepper

¼ cup thinly sliced green onions

2 egg whites, lightly beaten

1 egg, lightly beaten

2 tablespoons soy sauce

3 tablespoons peanut or vegetable oil, divided

1. Combine rice, bell pepper, green onions, egg whites, egg and soy sauce in medium bowl; mix well.

2. Heat 1 tablespoon oil in large nonstick skillet over medium heat. Spoon ⅓ cupfuls rice mixture into skillet; flatten slightly with back of spatula. Cook 3 to 4 minutes per side or until golden brown.* Repeat with remaining 2 tablespoons oil and rice mixture.

*To keep warm while preparing remaining patties, place on large baking sheet in 200°F oven.

TANGY RED CABBAGE WITH APPLES AND BACON

MAKES 4 SERVINGS

8 slices Irish or thick-cut bacon

1 large onion, sliced

½ small head red cabbage (1 pound), thinly sliced

1 tablespoon sugar

1 Granny Smith apple, peeled and sliced

2 tablespoons cider vinegar

½ teaspoon salt

¼ teaspoon black pepper

1. Cook bacon in large skillet over medium-high heat 6 to 8 minutes or until crisp, turning occasionally. Drain on paper towel-lined plate. Coarsely chop bacon.

2. Drain all but 2 tablespoons drippings from skillet. Add onion; cook and stir over medium-high heat 2 to 3 minutes or until onion begins to soften. Add cabbage and sugar; cook and stir 4 to 5 minutes or until cabbage wilts. Stir in apple; cook 3 minutes or until crisp-tender. Stir in vinegar; cook 1 minute or until absorbed.

3. Stir in bacon, salt and pepper; cook 1 minute or until heated through. Serve warm or at room temperature.

DRY-COOKED GREEN BEANS

MAKES 4 SERVINGS

4 ounces lean ground pork or turkey

2 tablespoons plus 1 teaspoon soy sauce, divided

2 tablespoons plus 1 teaspoon rice wine or dry sherry, divided

½ teaspoon dark sesame oil

2 tablespoons water

1 teaspoon sugar

3 cups vegetable oil

1 pound fresh green beans, trimmed and cut into 2-inch lengths

1 tablespoon sliced green onion

1. Combine pork, 1 teaspoon soy sauce, 1 teaspoon rice wine and sesame oil in medium bowl; mix well. Set aside.

2. Combine water, sugar, remaining 2 tablespoons soy sauce and 2 tablespoons rice wine in small bowl; mix well. Set aside.

3. Heat vegetable oil in large skillet over medium-high heat until oil registers 375°F on deep-fry thermometer. Carefully add half of beans; cook 2 to 3 minutes or until beans blister and are crisp-tender. Remove beans with slotted spoon to paper towels; drain. When oil returns to 375°F, repeat with remaining beans.

4. Pour off oil; heat skillet over medium-high heat 30 seconds. Add pork mixture; cook and stir 2 minutes or until well browned. Add beans and soy sauce mixture; toss until heated through. Transfer to serving dish. Sprinkle with green onion.

COUSCOUS PRIMAVERA

MAKES 4 SERVINGS

Nonstick cooking spray

1 shallot, minced *or* ¼ cup minced red onion

8 medium spears fresh asparagus, cooked and cut into 1-inch pieces

1 cup frozen peas

1 cup halved grape tomatoes

½ cup water

⅛ teaspoon salt

⅛ teaspoon black pepper

6 tablespoons uncooked whole wheat couscous

¼ cup grated Parmesan cheese

1. Spray large skillet with cooking spray; heat over medium heat. Add shallot; cook 3 minutes or until tender. Add asparagus and peas; cook 2 minutes or until peas are heated through. Add tomatoes; cook 2 minutes or until softened. Add water, salt and pepper; bring to a boil.

2. Stir in couscous. Reduce heat to low. Cover and simmer 2 minutes or until liquid is absorbed. Fluff with fork. Stir in cheese just before serving.

ASPARAGUS WITH NO-COOK CREAMY MUSTARD SAUCE

MAKES 6 SERVINGS

2 cups water

1½ pounds asparagus, trimmed

½ cup plain nonfat yogurt

2 tablespoons mayonnaise

1 tablespoon Dijon mustard

2 teaspoons lemon juice

½ teaspoon salt

Grated lemon peel (optional)

1. Bring water to a boil in large skillet over high heat. Add asparagus; return to a boil. Reduce heat; cover and simmer 3 minutes or until crisp-tender. Drain.

2. Meanwhile, whisk yogurt, mayonnaise, mustard, lemon juice and salt in small bowl until smooth and well blended.

3. Place asparagus on serving platter; top with sauce. Garnish with lemon peel.

CHARRED CORN SALAD

MAKES 6 SERVINGS

3 tablespoons fresh lime juice

½ teaspoon salt

¼ cup extra virgin olive oil

4 to 6 ears corn, husked (enough to make 3 to 4 cups kernels)

⅔ cup canned black beans, rinsed and drained

½ cup chopped fresh cilantro

2 teaspoons minced seeded chipotle pepper (1 canned chipotle pepper in adobo sauce *or* 1 dried chipotle pepper, reconstituted in boiling water)*

*Chipotle peppers can sting and irritate the skin, so wear rubber gloves when handling peppers and do not touch your eyes.

1. Whisk lime juice and salt in small bowl. Gradually whisk in oil until well blended. Set aside.

2. Cut corn kernels off cobs. Heat large skillet over medium-high heat. Cook corn in single layer 15 to 17 minutes or until browned and tender, turning frequently. Transfer to large plate to cool slightly. Place in medium bowl.

3. Place beans in small microwavable bowl; microwave on HIGH 1 minute or until heated through. Add beans, cilantro and chipotle pepper to corn; mix well. Pour lime juice mixture over corn mixture; stir to coat.

NOTE: Chipotle peppers in adobo sauce are available canned in the Mexican food section of most supermarkets. Since only a small amount is needed for this dish, spoon leftovers into a covered food storage container and refrigerate or freeze.

SKILLET SUCCOTASH

MAKES 4 SERVINGS

1 teaspoon canola oil

½ cup diced onion

½ cup diced green bell pepper

½ cup diced celery

½ teaspoon paprika

¾ cup frozen yellow or white corn

¾ cup frozen lima beans

½ cup canned diced tomatoes

1 teaspoon dried parsley flakes *or* 1 tablespoon minced fresh parsley

¼ teaspoon salt

¼ teaspoon black pepper

1. Heat oil in large skillet over medium heat. Add onion, bell pepper and celery; cook and stir 5 minutes or until onion is translucent and bell pepper and celery are crisp-tender. Stir in paprika.

2. Add corn, lima beans and tomatoes. Reduce heat. Cover and simmer 20 minutes or until beans are tender. Stir in parsley, salt and black pepper just before serving.

TIP: For additional flavor, add 1 clove minced garlic and 1 bay leaf. Remove and discard bay leaf before serving.

CARAMELIZED BRUSSELS SPROUTS WITH CRANBERRIES

MAKES 4 SERVINGS

1 tablespoon vegetable oil

1 pound Brussels sprouts, ends trimmed and discarded, thinly sliced

¼ cup dried cranberries

2 teaspoons packed brown sugar

¼ teaspoon salt

Heat oil in large skillet over medium-high heat. Add Brussels sprouts; cook and stir 10 minutes or until crisp-tender and beginning to brown. Add cranberries, brown sugar and salt; cook and stir 5 minutes or until browned.

SESAME SNOW PEAS

MAKES 4 SERVINGS

½ pound snow peas (Chinese pea pods)

2 teaspoons dark sesame oil

2 teaspoons vegetable oil

1 medium carrot, cut into matchstick pieces

2 green onions, cut into ¼-inch slices

½ teaspoon grated fresh ginger *or* ¼ teaspoon ground ginger

1 teaspoon soy sauce

1 tablespoon sesame seeds, toasted*

To toast sesame seeds, heat small skillet over medium heat. Add sesame seeds; cook and stir about 5 minutes or until golden.

1. To de-stem peas, pinch off stem end from each pod and pull strings down pod to remove, if present. (Young tender pods may have no strings.)

2. Heat large skillet over high heat. Add sesame and vegetable oils, swirling to coat sides. Heat oils until hot, about 30 seconds. Add snow peas, carrot, green onions and ginger; cook and stir 4 minutes or until peas are bright green and crisp-tender.

3. Stir in soy sauce. Transfer to warm serving dish; sprinkle with sesame seeds. Serve immediately.

MONTEREY POTATO HASH

MAKES 4 TO 6 SERVINGS

1 cup cherry tomatoes

2 tablespoons olive oil

4 small baking potatoes, unpeeled and cut into ¼-inch slices

1 medium red onion, sliced

2 cloves garlic, minced

1 teaspoon dried basil or oregano

¼ teaspoon salt

¼ teaspoon black pepper

1 cup water

1 large green bell pepper, halved and cut into ¼-inch slices

¼ cup (1 ounce) shredded Monterey Jack cheese

1. Rinse tomatoes and pat dry with paper towels. Cut tomatoes in half; set aside.

2. Heat large skillet over high heat 1 minute. Drizzle oil into skillet; heat 30 seconds. Add potatoes; cook and stir 8 minutes or until lightly browned. Reduce heat to medium. Add onion, garlic, basil, salt and black pepper; cook and stir 1 minute.

3. Stir in water; cover and cook 5 minutes or until potatoes are fork-tender, gently stirring once. Add bell pepper; cook and stir until water evaporates. Gently stir in tomatoes; cook until heated through. Transfer to serving dish; sprinkle with cheese.

SPANISH STEWED TOMATOES

MAKES 6 SERVINGS

- 2 tablespoons olive oil
- ½ teaspoon POLANER® Chopped Garlic
- 1 can (about 15 ounces) diced tomatoes
- ½ cup water
- 1 packet (1.25 ounces) ORTEGA® Taco Seasoning Mix
- 2 cups frozen green beans
- 2 tablespoons ORTEGA® Fire-Roasted Diced Green Chiles

HEAT oil in medium skillet over medium heat until hot. Add garlic. Cook and stir until golden brown. Stir in tomatoes, water and taco seasoning mix. Simmer 3 minutes. Add beans and chiles; simmer 4 minutes or until beans are heated through.

VARIATION: Replace the green beans with corn or lima beans.

SOUTHERN-STYLE SUCCOTASH

MAKES 6 SERVINGS

2 tablespoons butter

1 cup chopped onion

1 package (10 ounces) frozen lima beans, thawed

1 cup frozen corn, thawed

½ cup chopped red bell pepper

1 can (about 15 ounces) hominy, rinsed and drained

⅓ cup chicken broth

½ teaspoon salt

¼ teaspoon hot pepper sauce

¼ cup chopped green onion tops or fresh chives

1. Melt butter in large nonstick skillet over medium heat. Add onion; cook and stir 5 minutes. Add lima beans, corn and bell pepper; cook and stir 5 minutes.

2. Add hominy, broth, salt and hot pepper sauce; simmer 5 minutes or until most liquid is evaporated. Remove from heat; stir in chopped green onions before serving.

GREEN BEANS AND SHIITAKE MUSHROOMS

MAKES 4 TO 6 SERVINGS

10 to 12 dried shiitake mushrooms (about 1 ounce)

¾ cup water, divided

3 tablespoons oyster sauce

1 tablespoon cornstarch

4 cloves garlic, minced

⅛ teaspoon red pepper flakes

1 tablespoon vegetable oil

¾ to 1 pound fresh green beans

⅓ cup slivered fresh basil or chopped fresh cilantro

2 green onions, sliced diagonally

⅓ cup roasted peanuts

1. Place mushrooms in bowl; cover with hot water. Let stand 30 minutes or until caps are soft. Drain mushrooms; squeeze out excess water. Remove and discard stems. Slice caps into thin strips.

2. Combine ¼ cup water, oyster sauce, cornstarch, garlic and red pepper flakes in small bowl; mix well. Set aside.

3. Heat oil in medium skillet over medium-high heat. Add mushrooms, beans and remaining ½ cup water; cook and stir until water boils. Reduce heat to medium-low. Cover; cook 8 to 10 minutes or until beans are crisp-tender, stirring occasionally.

4. Stir cornstarch mixture; add to skillet. Cook and stir until sauce thickens and coats beans. (If cooking water has evaporated, add enough water to form thick sauce.) Top with basil, green onions and peanuts; mix well. Transfer to serving bowl.

CREAMY CORN AND VEGETABLE ORZO

MAKES 6 SERVINGS

2 tablespoons butter

4 medium green onions, sliced (about ½ cup)

2 cups frozen whole kernel corn

1 package (10 ounces) frozen vegetables (chopped broccoli, peas, sliced carrots **or** cut green beans)

½ of a 16-ounce package rice-shaped pasta (orzo), cooked and drained

1 can (10¾ ounces) Campbell's® Condensed Cream of Celery Soup (Regular **or** 98% Fat Free)

½ cup water

1. Heat the butter in a 12-inch skillet over medium heat. Add the green onions and cook until tender. Add the corn, vegetables and pasta. Cook and stir for 3 minutes.

2. Stir the soup and water into the skillet. Cook and stir for 5 minutes or until mixture is hot and bubbling. Serve immediately.

CHINESE VEGETABLES

MAKES 6 TO 8 SERVINGS

1 pound fresh broccoli

1½ teaspoons vegetable oil

2 medium yellow onions, cut into wedges and separated

2 cloves garlic, minced

1½ tablespoons minced fresh ginger

8 ounces fresh spinach, coarsely chopped

4 stalks celery, diagonally cut into ½-inch pieces

8 ounces fresh snow peas *or* 1 package (6 ounces) thawed frozen snow peas, trimmed and strings removed

4 medium carrots, sliced

8 green onions, diagonally cut into thin slices

¾ cup chicken broth

1 tablespoon soy sauce

Hot cooked rice

1. Cut broccoli tops into florets. Cut stalks into 2×¼-inch strips.

2. Heat oil in wok or large nonstick skillet over high heat. Add broccoli stalks, yellow onions, garlic and ginger; stir-fry 1 minute. Add broccoli florets, spinach, celery, snow peas, carrots and green onions; toss lightly.

3. Add broth and soy sauce to vegetables; toss to coat. Bring to a boil; cover and cook 2 to 3 minutes or until vegetables are crisp-tender. Serve over rice.

DAZZLING DESSERTS

CINNAMON ROLL-TOPPED PEACH AND RASPBERRY COBBLER

MAKES 8 SERVINGS

1 package (16 ounces) frozen peaches, thawed and drained

1 package (12 ounces) frozen raspberries, thawed and drained

½ cup sugar

¼ cup quick-cooking tapioca

¼ cup water

2 teaspoons vanilla

1 teaspoon salt

1 package (about 12 ounces) refrigerated cinnamon rolls with icing

1. Preheat oven to 350°F. Combine peaches, raspberries, sugar, tapioca, water, vanilla and salt in large ovenproof skillet; stir to blend. Top with cinnamon rolls.

2. Bake 40 to 45 minutes or until golden brown. Drizzle with icing; serve warm.

CINNAMON DESSERT TACOS WITH FRUIT SALSA

MAKES 6 SERVINGS

1 cup sliced fresh strawberries

1 cup cubed fresh pineapple

1 cup cubed peeled kiwi

½ teaspoon minced jalapeño pepper*

4 tablespoons plus 1 teaspoon sugar

1 tablespoon ground cinnamon

6 (8-inch) flour tortillas

Nonstick cooking spray

*Jalapeño peppers can sting and irritate the skin, so wear rubber gloves when handling peppers and do not touch your eyes.

1. Combine strawberries, pineapple, kiwi, jalapeño pepper and 1 tablespoon plus 1 teaspoon sugar in large bowl; stir to blend. Set aside. Combine remaining 3 tablespoons sugar and cinnamon in small bowl; set aside.

2. Spray tortilla lightly on both sides with cooking spray. Heat over medium heat in nonstick skillet until slightly puffed and golden brown. Remove from heat; immediately dust both sides with cinnamon-sugar mixture. Shake excess cinnamon-sugar back into bowl. Repeat until all tortillas are warmed.

3. Fill tortillas with fruit mixture and fold in half. Serve immediately.

HOT SKILLET PINEAPPLE ORANGE SNACK CAKE

MAKES 8 SERVINGS

1 can (8 ounces) crushed pineapple in juice, undrained

1 cup orange juice, divided

2 tablespoons firmly packed dark brown sugar

1⅓ cups all-purpose flour

¼ cup granulated sugar

¼ cup powdered nonfat milk

2 teaspoons baking powder

½ teaspoon grated orange peel

3 egg whites

2 tablespoons canola oil

1 teaspoon vanilla

1. Preheat oven to 350°F.

2. Drain pineapple in fine mesh strainer, reserving liquid. Place 10-inch skillet over high heat. Add pineapple juice and ½ cup orange juice. Bring to a boil; continue boiling 2½ minutes or until liquid measures ¼ cup. Remove skillet from heat; add brown sugar to measured liquid in skillet. Stir until blended. Using teaspoon, spoon pineapple evenly over brown-sugar mixture. *Do not stir.* Set aside.

3. Combine flour, granulated sugar, powdered milk, baking powder and orange peel in medium bowl; stir to blend. Add remaining ½ cup orange juice, egg whites, oil and vanilla. Beat on low speed with electric mixer until blended. Increase to medium speed. Beat 2 minutes or until smooth. Spoon batter evenly over pineapple mixture in skillet.

4. Bake 30 to 35 minutes or until toothpick inserted into center comes out clean. Place on cooling rack 5 minutes. Loosen edges with knife and place plate over skillet. Invert, scraping any remaining pineapple from skillet and spooning on top of cake. Cut into eight wedges and serve warm.

CHOCOLATE CRÊPES WITH STRAWBERRY FILLING

MAKES 8 CRÊPES (ABOUT 4 SERVINGS)

1 cup all-purpose flour

⅔ cup low-fat (1%) milk

2 egg whites

1 egg

3 tablespoons sugar

3 tablespoons unsweetened cocoa powder

1 tablespoon butter, melted and cooled

½ teaspoon salt

2 teaspoons canola oil

3 tablespoons strawberry fruit spread

3½ cups sliced fresh or thawed frozen strawberries

½ cup thawed frozen whipped topping

Fresh mint leaves (optional)

1. Combine flour, milk, egg whites, egg, sugar, cocoa, butter and salt in large bowl; whisk until smooth and well blended.

2. Brush medium nonstick skillet with ¼ teaspoon oil; heat over medium heat. Pour about ¼ cup batter into center of pan. Immediately pick up pan and swirl to coat with batter. Cook 1 minute or until crêpe is dull on top and edges are dry. Turn and cook 30 seconds. Remove to plate; repeat with remaining oil and batter.

3. Stir strawberry fruit spread in medium bowl until softened. Add strawberries; toss to coat.

4. Spoon about ¼ cup strawberry mixture down center of each crêpe; roll up to enclose filling. Top each serving with 2 tablespoons whipped topping. Garnish with mint.

SAUTÉED APPLES SUPREME

MAKES 2 SERVINGS

2 small apples *or* 1 large apple

1 teaspoon butter

¼ cup unsweetened apple juice or cider

2 teaspoons packed brown sugar

½ teaspoon ground cinnamon

⅔ cup vanilla ice cream or frozen yogurt (optional)

1 tablespoon chopped walnuts, toasted

1. Cut apples into quarters; remove cores and cut into ½-inch-thick slices.

2. Melt butter in large nonstick skillet over medium heat. Add apples; cook 4 minutes, stirring occasionally.

3. Combine apple juice, brown sugar and cinnamon in small bowl; pour over apples. Simmer 5 minutes or until apples are tender and sauce thickens. Transfer to serving bowls; serve with ice cream, if desired. Sprinkle with walnuts.

SO-EASY PEACH PIE

MAKES 8 SERVINGS

- 1 package (16 ounces) frozen unsweetened peach slices, thawed, juice reserved
- 2 teaspoons cornstarch
- ½ cup golden raisins
- 4 tablespoons sugar, divided

- 1 teaspoon vanilla or almond extract
- ¼ teaspoon ground cinnamon (optional)
- 1 prepared pie crust (half of 15-ounce package)

1. Combine peach juice and cornstarch in large nonstick skillet; stir until cornstarch is dissolved. Add peaches and raisins; bring to a boil over high heat. Boil 2 minutes, stirring occasionally. Remove from heat; stir in 3 tablespoons sugar, vanilla and cinnamon, if desired.

2. Slide baked crust over peach mixture in skillet. Sprinkle with remaining 1 tablespoon sugar.

APPLE-RASPBERRY GRANOLA SKILLET

MAKES 8 SERVINGS

- 1 cup granola without raisins
- 2 tablespoons water
- 1 tablespoon lemon juice
- 2 teaspoons cornstarch
- 1 pound apples, cored and sliced
- ½ teaspoon ground cinnamon
- 4 ounces frozen unsweetened raspberries
- 2 tablespoons sugar
- ½ teaspoon vanilla
- ¼ teaspoon almond extract

1. Place granola in small resealable food storage bag; seal tightly. Crush to coarse crumb texture; set aside.

2. Combine water, lemon juice and cornstarch in small bowl; stir until cornstarch is completely dissolved.

3. Combine apples, cornstarch mixture and cinnamon in 10-inch skillet; stir until blended. Heat over medium-high heat. Bring to a boil. Boil 1 minute or until thickened, stirring constantly.

4. Remove skillet from heat. Gently fold in raspberries, sugar, vanilla and almond extract. Sprinkle granola crumbs evenly over top. Let stand, uncovered, 30 minutes.

SWEET AND SPICY BANANAS FOSTER

MAKES 4 SERVINGS

½ cup (1 stick) butter

½ cup firmly packed light brown sugar

2 tablespoons ORTEGA® Taco Seasoning Mix

4 bananas, peeled, halved and cut in half lengthwise

¼ cup dark rum

Vanilla ice cream

MELT butter in large skillet over medium heat. Stir in brown sugar; cook and stir until smooth and sugar has dissolved. Stir in taco seasoning mix.

ADD banana quarters; swirl around in skillet to coat bananas completely. Add rum; simmer 4 minutes or until alcohol has cooked out.

PLACE ice cream in serving dishes. Arrange 4 banana pieces in each dish; spoon sauce over ice cream and bananas.

SERVING SUGGESTIONS: For a warmer treat, serve this sweet and spicy version of Bananas Foster over pound cake or your favorite coffee cake.

HONEY SOPAIPILLAS

MAKES 16 SOPAIPILLAS

- ¼ cup plus 2 teaspoons sugar, divided
- ½ teaspoon ground cinnamon
- 2 cups all-purpose flour
- ½ teaspoon salt
- 2 teaspoons baking powder
- 2 tablespoons shortening
- ¾ cup warm water
- Vegetable oil for deep-frying
- Honey

1. Combine ¼ cup sugar and cinnamon in small bowl; set aside. Combine remaining 2 teaspoons sugar, flour, salt and baking powder in large bowl. Cut in shortening with pastry blender or two knives until mixture resembles fine crumbs. Gradually add water; stir with fork until mixture forms dough. Turn out onto lightly floured surface; knead 2 minutes or until smooth. Shape into a ball; cover with bowl and let rest 30 minutes.

2. Divide dough into four equal portions; shape each into a ball. Flatten each ball into 8-inch circle, ⅛ inch thick. Cut each round into four wedges.

3. Pour oil into deep skillet to depth of 1½ inches. Heat to 360°F. Cook dough, two pieces at a time, 2 minutes or until puffed and golden brown, turning once during cooking. Remove from oil with slotted spoon; drain on paper towels. Sprinkle with cinnamon-sugar mixture. Repeat with remaining sopaipillas. Serve hot with honey.

PEAR TORTETTA

MAKES 8 SERVINGS

- ⅓ cup granulated sugar
- ⅓ cup packed brown sugar
- ½ teaspoon ground cinnamon
- 4 medium ripe pears, peeled, cored and cut in half
- 2 tablespoons lemon juice
- 3 tablespoons margarine, softened
- ½ of a 17.3-ounce package Pepperidge Farm® Puff Pastry Sheets (1 sheet), thawed

1. Heat the oven to 425°F. Stir the granulated sugar, brown sugar and cinnamon in a small bowl. Brush the pears with the lemon juice.

2. Spread the margarine in a 10-inch oven-safe skillet. Sprinkle with the sugar mixture. Arrange the pear halves in the skillet, cut-side up, with the tapered end of the pears towards the center of the skillet. Cook over medium heat for 8 minutes or until the sugar mixture is thickened. Remove the skillet from the heat.

3. Unfold the pastry sheet on a lightly floured surface. Roll the pastry sheet into a 13-inch circle. Place the pastry over the pears and tuck in the sides lightly around the pears.

4. Bake for 25 minutes or until the pastry is golden brown. Cool in the skillet on a wire rack for 5 minutes. Carefully invert the tortetta onto a serving plate.

KITCHEN TIP: When inverting the tortetta, make sure to use oven mitts and hold the skillet and plate firmly together. If any pears stick to the skillet, just remove them and arrange them on the tortetta.

CINNAMON TORTILLA WITH CREAM CHEESE & STRAWBERRIES

MAKES 1 SERVING

2 teaspoons sugar

⅛ teaspoon ground cinnamon

1 (6-inch) flour tortilla

Nonstick cooking spray

1 tablespoon soft cream cheese

⅓ cup fresh strawberry slices

1. Combine sugar and cinnamon in small bowl; mix well. Heat large nonstick skillet over medium heat.

2. Lightly spray one side of tortilla with cooking spray; sprinkle with cinnamon mixture.

3. Place tortilla, cinnamon side down, in hot skillet. Cook 2 minutes or until lightly browned. Remove from skillet.

4. Spread uncooked side of tortilla with cream cheese; arrange strawberries down center of tortilla. Roll up tortilla, or fold, to serve.

TIP: Prepare recipe through step 3. Mash a few of the strawberry slices with a fork until almost smooth; stir into cream cheese. Proceed as directed in step 4.

CHOCOLATE CHIP SKILLET COOKIE

MAKES 8 SERVINGS

1¾ cups all-purpose flour

1 teaspoon baking soda

1 teaspoon salt

¾ cup (1½ sticks) butter, softened

¾ cup packed brown sugar

½ cup granulated sugar

2 eggs

1 teaspoon vanilla

1 package (12 ounces) semisweet chocolate chips

Sea salt (optional)

Ice cream (optional)

1. Preheat oven to 350°F.

2. Combine flour, baking soda and salt in medium bowl. Beat butter, brown sugar and granulated sugar in large bowl with electric mixer at medium speed until creamy. Beat in eggs and vanilla until well blended. Gradually beat in flour mixture at low speed just until blended. Stir in chocolate chips. Press batter evenly into large skillet. Sprinkle lightly with sea salt, if desired.

3. Bake 35 minutes or until top and edges are golden brown but cookie is still soft in center. Cool on wire rack 10 minutes before cutting into wedges. Serve warm with ice cream, if desired.

APPLE CRANBERRY CRUMBLE

MAKES 4 SERVINGS

4 large apples (about 1⅓ pounds), peeled and cut into ¼-inch slices

2 cups fresh or frozen cranberries

⅓ cup granulated sugar

6 tablespoons all-purpose flour, divided

1 teaspoon apple pie spice, divided

¼ teaspoon salt, divided

½ cup chopped walnuts

¼ cup old-fashioned oats

2 tablespoons packed brown sugar

¼ cup (½ stick) butter, cut into small pieces

1. Preheat oven to 375°F.

2. Combine apples, cranberries, granulated sugar, 2 tablespoons flour, ½ teaspoon apple pie spice and ⅛ teaspoon salt in large bowl; toss to coat. Spoon into medium skillet.

3. Combine remaining 4 tablespoons flour, walnuts, oats, brown sugar, remaining ½ teaspoon apple pie spice and ⅛ teaspoon salt in medium bowl; mix well. Cut in butter with pastry blender or two knives until mixture resembles coarse crumbs. Sprinkle over fruit mixture in skillet.

4. Bake 50 to 60 minutes or until filling is bubbly and topping is lightly browned.

POACHED PEARS IN CINNAMON-APRICOT SAUCE

MAKES 4 SERVINGS

1 can (5½ ounces) apricot nectar

1 tablespoon sugar

1 teaspoon lemon juice

½ teaspoon ground cinnamon

¼ teaspoon grated lemon peel

⅛ teaspoon ground cloves

2 large pears

Whipped topping (optional)

1. Combine apricot nectar, sugar, lemon juice, cinnamon, lemon peel and cloves in large skillet. Bring to a boil over medium-high heat.

2. Meanwhile, cut pears lengthwise into halves, leaving stem attached to one half. Remove cores. Cut pears lengthwise into thin slices, taking care not to cut through stem end. Add pears to skillet with nectar mixture; return to a boil. Reduce heat to medium-low. Simmer, covered, 6 to 8 minutes or just until pears are tender. Carefully remove pears from skillet, reserving liquid.

3. Simmer liquid in skillet, uncovered, over medium heat 2 to 3 minutes or until mixture thickens slightly, stirring occasionally. Fan out pears; spoon sauce over pears. Serve pears warm or chilled with whipped topping, if desired.

SWEET 'N' EASY FRUIT CRISP BOWLS

MAKES 2 SERVINGS

2 tablespoons granola with almonds

Nonstick cooking spray

1 red apple (8 ounces), such as Gala, diced into ½-inch pieces

1 tablespoon dried sweetened cranberries

¼ teaspoon apple pie spice or ground cinnamon

1 teaspoon butter

2 teaspoons sugar

¼ teaspoon almond extract

2 tablespoons vanilla ice cream

1. Place granola in small resealable food storage bag; crush lightly to form coarse crumbs. Set aside. Spray large skillet with cooking spray; heat over medium heat. Add apples, cranberries and apple pie spice; cook 4 minutes or until apples are just tender, stirring frequently.

2. Remove from heat, stir in butter, sugar and almond extract. Spoon into two dessert bowls. Sprinkle with granola; top with ice cream. Serve immediately.

NOTE: You may make the apple mixture up to 8 hours in advance and top with granola and ice cream at time of serving. To rewarm crisp, microwave apple mixture (before adding granola and ice cream) on HIGH 20 to 30 seconds or until slightly heated.

CARAMELIZED PINEAPPLE

MAKES 4 SERVINGS

1 tablespoon butter

2 cups fresh pineapple chunks

3 tablespoons sugar

¾ cup vanilla frozen yogurt

1. Spray baking sheet with nonstick cooking spray.

2. Melt butter in large nonstick skillet over medium-high heat. Add pineapple and sugar; cook and stir 10 to 12 minutes or until pineapple is golden brown. Spread on prepared baking sheet. Cool 5 minutes.

3. Spoon pineapple into four dessert dishes. Top each serving evenly with frozen yogurt. Serve immediately.

INDEX

page 93

page 56

page 14

ACKNOWLEDGMENTS

The publisher would like to thank the companies and organization listed below for the use of their recipes and photographs in this publication.

The Beef Checkoff

Bob Evans®

Butterball® Turkey

Campbell Soup Company

The Golden Grain Company®

Hormel Foods, LLC

Johnsonville Sausage, LLC

Ortega®, A Division of B&G Foods North America, Inc.

METRIC CONVERSION CHART

VOLUME MEASUREMENTS (dry)

1/8 teaspoon = 0.5 mL
1/4 teaspoon = 1 mL
1/2 teaspoon = 2 mL
3/4 teaspoon = 4 mL
1 teaspoon = 5 mL
1 tablespoon = 15 mL
2 tablespoons = 30 mL
1/4 cup = 60 mL
1/3 cup = 75 mL
1/2 cup = 125 mL
2/3 cup = 150 mL
3/4 cup = 175 mL
1 cup = 250 mL
2 cups = 1 pint = 500 mL
3 cups = 750 mL
4 cups = 1 quart = 1 L

VOLUME MEASUREMENTS (fluid)

1 fluid ounce (2 tablespoons) = 30 mL
4 fluid ounces (1/2 cup) = 125 mL
8 fluid ounces (1 cup) = 250 mL
12 fluid ounces (1 1/2 cups) = 375 mL
16 fluid ounces (2 cups) = 500 mL

WEIGHTS (mass)

1/2 ounce = 15 g
1 ounce = 30 g
3 ounces = 90 g
4 ounces = 120 g
8 ounces = 225 g
10 ounces = 285 g
12 ounces = 360 g
16 ounces = 1 pound = 450 g

DIMENSIONS

1/16 inch = 2 mm
1/8 inch = 3 mm
1/4 inch = 6 mm
1/2 inch = 1.5 cm
3/4 inch = 2 cm
1 inch = 2.5 cm

OVEN TEMPERATURES

250°F = 120°C
275°F = 140°C
300°F = 150°C
325°F = 160°C
350°F = 180°C
375°F = 190°C
400°F = 200°C
425°F = 220°C
450°F = 230°C

BAKING PAN SIZES

Utensil	Size in Inches/Quarts	Metric Volume	Size in Centimeters
Baking or Cake Pan (square or rectangular)	8×8×2	2 L	20×20×5
	9×9×2	2.5 L	23×23×5
	12×8×2	3 L	30×20×5
	13×9×2	3.5 L	33×23×5
Loaf Pan	8×4×3	1.5 L	20×10×7
	9×5×3	2 L	23×13×7
Round Layer Cake Pan	8×1½	1.2 L	20×4
	9×1½	1.5 L	23×4
Pie Plate	8×1¼	750 mL	20×3
	9×1¼	1 L	23×3
Baking Dish or Casserole	1 quart	1 L	—
	1½ quart	1.5 L	—
	2 quart	2 L	—